THE SEEKING SELF

THE SEEKING SELF

The Quest for
Self Improvement
and the Creation of
Personal Suffering

RICHARD E. LIND

PHANES PRESS

Published by Phanes Press, PO Box 6114, Grand Rapids, Michigan 49516, USA

www.phanes.com

Library of Congress Cataloging in Publication Data

Lind, Richard E.
    The seeking self : the quest for self improvement and the creation of personal suffering / by Richard E. Lind
        p. cm.
    Includes bibliographical references and index.
    ISBN 1-890482-76-5 (pbk. : alk. paper)
    1. Self-help techniques. 2. Self-destructive behavior.   I. Title.

BF632 .L56 2000
155.2'5--dc21   00-058873

This book is printed on alkaline paper which conforms to the permanent paper standard developed by the National Information Standards Organization.

06   05   04   03   02   01   2000   1   2   3   4   5   6   7

Printed and bound in the United States of America.

Contents

CONTENTS

It is possible to fall into the heights,
as well as into the depths.

—Hölderlin

Introduction

apodictic style

SEEKING some type of radical improvement, transcendence, or transformation of the self comes highly recommended in both Eastern and Western cultures, and especially in American culture.[1] But this recommendation is based on the fundamental misconception that the self can achieve perfection or voluntarily transcend or transform itself.

I agree

When transformation of the self occurs, it is never a result of successful seeking, but always a result of its failure. Nearly all spiritual disciplines oriented toward the goals of transcendence and self-transformation are misleading. That is because they prevent rather than foster the achievement of these goals by fostering preoccupation with the illusion of spiritual self-mastery and the control of one's destiny.

agree

Seeking radical self-improvement, perfection, or transcendence is not only the chief obstacle to spiritual attainment, but has also been one of the most common causes of chronic suffering and ruined lives throughout history. By its very nature, the quest for transcendence or perfection ensnares the self in egoism, a false, heroic sense of unity and efficacy, and chronic internal conflict. Consequently, the one element common to all serious seeking after self-realization and transcendence is suffering, caused by the disintegration of the seeking self.

agree

This self-inflicted suffering of the seeker cannot be avoided by

absolutist thinking

any discipline or technique, but is rather the product of these avoidant practices. The modern self, habituated from birth to engage in seeking, can begin to reduce its self-inflicted suffering only by discovering that its integrity, if not its sanity, has been fundamentally compromised by the futility of its own seeking. An end of this suffering can occur only after the painful discovery of the self's inability to radically change itself.

Yet, paradoxically, an individual's growing realization of his or her powerlessness to achieve radical self-improvement or transcendence often goads the self into even more frantic seeking, despite the increasing apparent futility of these efforts. For all too many, a tragic circular trap of suffering, followed by futile seeking to heal the resulting open wound, is then compulsively repeated until the onset of chronic depression, other mental illnesses, or death.

Everything the self does in the service of seeking self-realization or transcendence prevents psychic reintegration. Modern culture assists in the prevention of reintegration by habituating the self to depend upon self-destructive seeking to the point that it is unable to give it up. No alternatives are offered, and the self rightly fears that it will cease to exist if it does not continue to seek to improve itself. Escape from this entrapment is only possible by means of the relatively rare occurrence of an involuntary reintegration of the conflicting parts of the psyche, which sometimes follows the exhaustion of self-interested seeking. In this unusual circumstance, self-transformation or integration occurs in spite of the seeking of the self, not because of it.

An alternative to the rare occurrence of involuntary reintegration is the voluntary giving up of seeking, which may be neither possible nor desirable if it results in severe depression and defeat. But facing this alternative may nevertheless be preferable to an endless cycle of resurrecting and then tearing apart the seeking self and the psyche as a whole. This self-destructive behavior is at least as old as the Egyptian myths of the dismemberment of Osiris and of his Greek equivalent, Dionysus, but less is understood about it now than was common knowledge five thousand years ago. To understand the context of this behavior and the choice of refusing to let oneself continue to be a sacrificial victim, it is crucial to distinguish between the goal of reintegration versus goals that encourage the pursuit of perfection or transcendence.

If wholeness or reunification of the psyche is the ultimate goal of seeking, this goal is subverted by the quest for transcendence or perfection, which results in divisiveness—the opposite condition of that which is being sought. In the same way that love cannot be achieved through hate, unity cannot be achieved through divisiveness, even though these negative states may be necessary preludes to reunification and complete self-acceptance.

Giving up the quest for self-realization and transcendence does not mean that the goal of reintegration is abandoned, but rather that integration is recognized as the only realistic alternative. But integration or self-transformation, like the goals of self-realization and transcendence, cannot be achieved through self-interested striving. Nonetheless, understanding how and why reintegration occurs may help reorient the self toward a healing self-awareness—an awareness that includes the ability to choose between seeking and its alternative.

In this book, my aim is to counterbalance the overly positive view of seeking in contemporary thought, psychology, and spirituality, by explaining why suffering, failure, and disintegration always accompany the dedicated seeking of self-realization and transcendence. The suffering of the seeker is a message, and those who fully understand this message must finally realize that the cure for their ills is not to be found in seeking ideal goals or spiritual perfection, but rather in the reintegration of the psyche.

Although this book is written from a psychological perspective, I have included "wisdom samples" from various spiritual traditions that support and throw further light on the points I am trying to make. Also included are historical examples and case histories that illustrate how these themes play themselves out in the lives of individuals.

present

Wisdom Sample 1

IN THE earliest Pali texts of Buddhist scripture, the notion of *nirvana* or enlightenment was described as the solution to a complex of problems, the foremost being universal suffering. The primary cause of suffering, and one of the chief obstacles to enlightenment, was belief in an unchanging, permanent soul or self. This delusion of a separate self resulted in a split in the psyche and in bondage: "To Buddhism, the illusion of a separate self is original sin. It is the cause of evil, of death, and of all the sorrows to which mortals are heir."[2] As Mark Epstein writes,

> In the Buddhist view, a realized being has realized her own lack of true self. She is present by virtue of her absence and can function effectively and spontaneously in the world precisely because of her ability to see the self as already broken ... it may be the absence of grasping for that essential core that unleashes the flood of affect that makes us feel most real.[3]

Nirvana was achieved by a "settling in the heart,"[4] but could only be realized by an individual freed from the obsessions of the self. The *arahant*, the individual who had achieved nirvana, was "free from the emotions and desires by which egoism and attachment are created"; and because he had "laid down the burden," he knew that "there is nothing more to be done."[5] The arahant was without desire for action and life, had passed beyond good and evil, had no false hope, and never consciously tried to achieve anything.

Nirvana was described with the following words and phrases: the rejection of all attachment, destruction of craving and of the obsessions, freedom from desire, freedom from the pride "I am," the cessation of becoming, the calming of all activities, stopping, emptying, to be extinguished, release, freedom from sorrow, happiness, security, and peace of mind.

Almost 1500 years after the early Pali texts, Shinran (1173–1263 C.E.), a disciple of Honen, who founded Pure Land Buddhism, claimed that no act undertaken by human beings could bring them to enlightenment. True reality was described as *jinen* (working "of itself"), or wisdom-compassion, actively bringing beings to awakening without any contrivance on their part. Shinran named wisdom-compassion the "Other-power," as opposed to self-power, or reliance on one's own mastery of practices and disciplines.

Self-power manifested a fundamental self-attachment in which one sought to attain rebirth through one's own effort. Genuine engagement on the correct path arose when such calculation was overturned and abandoned. All judgments of good and evil, and associated acts believed to promote or prevent enlightenment, were false and useless, being inevitably distorted and made ineffective by egocentricity. It was precisely when the efforts of the egocentric self to move itself toward awakening fell away that true reality approached.

Chapter 1

The Problem of Seeking

SERIOUS SEEKERS of self-realization and transcendence are usually discontented and disillusioned with life, and blame themselves for their disturbing situation. Discontent motivates a strong desire to quickly and radically change the self, to erase embarrassing faults and failures, and to find a way to transcend the sorrows and futility of existence. Disillusionment results in a need to recreate a credible belief that life will, after all, be rewarding and meaningful.

Under these negative circumstances, it is natural to look for a cure, a belief system, and discipline that will end discontent and hopelessness. There have always been a variety of traditional, marginal, and radical "cures" for the suffering of the discontented and disillusioned. Each system offers various beliefs and disciplines, and claims its methods to be reliable means for obtaining ideal outcomes. But there have also been critics of these "cures" throughout Western history.

For the ancient Greeks, recognition and acceptance of one's fate was the first and most important step toward experiencing the good life. To attempt to alter one's fate was impious, dangerous, and bound to provoke the wrath of the gods. Theognis (sixth century B.C.E.) summarized this point of view as follows: "We are helpless: It is hard: but we are caught and confined. We are men, what we think is vanity, for we know nothing. All is disposed of by the gods in the way they wish."[1] Simonides (*c.* 500 B.C.E.) elaborated on this point of view:

> Any man is good while his luck is good,
> bad when bad, and for the most part
> they are best whom the gods love.
> Therefore, I will not throw away my
> time and life into unprofitable hope
> and emptiness, the search for that
> object which cannot possibly be . . .
> For the generation of fools is
> endless.[2]

The later Epicurean, Skeptic, and Stoic philosophers (*c.* 350 B.C.E.–200 C.E.) of Greece and Rome understood suffering to be the consequence of "false beliefs" and "empty striving." The cure of suffering was to stop believing in, and stop seeking after, unrealistic ideals—those illusory cultural and spiritual goals that falsely promised the attainment of happiness and the end of suffering. For these philosophers, the suspension of judgment, false hopes, and empty striving was the only way to achieve *ataraxia* or peace of mind.

Similarly in the Christian tradition, the sin of pride or sanctimonious seeking came to be identified as the primary sin, and the gateway to all other sins. To seek perfection or salvation was to turn away in prideful abandonment of submission to God. It was an attempt to usurp the governance of God over the soul and replace it with the governance of the personal conscience. But no matter how well-informed the conscience was about religious law and communal ethics, this was no substitute for the gift of grace. For through the experience of grace, God's love was freely given, and not won by human striving.   *so obey the Pope, worm!*

Over the last few centuries, however, with the liberalization of Christianity and the secularization of society, even the minority of traditional religious critics of seeking have disappeared. The seeker is currently confronted with a Babylonian feast of religious and secular prescriptions for positive change. Each claims to provide the one true way to the one true goal, and each of them says: "If you identify with these beliefs and dutifully perform these disciplines, you will live happily ever after, and here are some testimonials to prove it." Yet, while new disciplines of self-realization seem to work for a few individuals, there are diminishing returns as enthusiasm wanes and it becomes clear that these individuals are the exceptions rather than the rule.

Within the last twenty years, the psychology section in bookstores has often been renamed or supplemented by a self-help section. This change of emphasis reflects the unmet needs and untreated symptoms of modern individuals, as the current therapeutic establishment has become increasingly unresponsive to many of the concerns addressed by the self-help literature—in particular, to the pursuit of various prescriptions for the attainment of self-realization and transcendence by the "worried well."

This type of self-help literature has been readily available and popular for several centuries, and its content has not significantly changed since the late nineteenth century. Its rhetoric introduces seemingly new spiritual concepts and techniques, and embeds these concepts in both secular, "scientific" language, and in the language of traditional and esoteric religions. Based on the claim

Overgeneralization fallacy

of being a new discovery or method, radical promises of ideal outcomes are made. But few if any of these concepts and techniques are new, and without exception they are almost entirely useless for the pursuit of self-transformation except as elaborate diversions and placebos. In most cases, these pseudo-solutions are ultimately harmful to those who take them seriously.

In this self-help culture of individual seekers, psychological development and progress are portrayed as self-initiated and self-sustained through practical disciplines contained in "how-to" manuals promising the attainment of whatever type of ideal goal one chooses to pursue. This literature promotes the idea that one need only follow certain practices and disciplines and attainment of the good life will naturally follow. Self-help literature is based on the assumption that efforts toward self-improvement are usually effective and worthwhile, and for some limited goals, such as diet, exercise, or relaxation, this may sometimes be true. But the majority of the claims and promised benefits, especially those oriented toward self-realization and transcendence, are overstated and misleading.

Seekers should beware of those claiming to offer disciplines and practices that produce radical, positive change. All of these claims are false because there is no method, practice, or discipline through which to reliably and predictably achieve self-realization, transcendence, or reintegration.

Those who claim to have found self-realization or transcendence and then attempt to convince others of their self-serving interpretation of their experience (and those who for various reasons attempt to recruit others into their self-created disciplines for achieving these goals), are misleading their potential followers.

This is due to the false assumption that their followers can repro-
duce the point of view and alleged success acquired by these self-
appointed authorities. But neither transcendence, perfection, or
transformation can ever result from imitation. To seek to become
one's or someone else's ideal has always been, and will continue to
be, a path of self-destruction.

Those who cannot or will not give up seeking remain trapped
in their dependence upon successful performance to justify their
sense of personal worth, their self-esteem. Their resistance is
natural and a sign of where they are in the process—that is, caught
up in the errant belief that they are building up the self, rather than
realizing that they are tearing it apart. Even though faintly recognizing that resistance toward accepting "who" and "what" they
are is futile, their "empty-striving" remains compulsive, a survival
issue, out of the bounds of voluntary choice and control.

Inappropriate, excessive seeking in its various forms is one of
the root causes of the ills of both modern individuals and modern
society. In American culture, compulsive seeking is not only
common, but expected. Rather than fostering stability and acceptance, however, compulsive seeking easily becomes short-sighted,
destructive, and goads individuals to excess. But many seekers
have never suffered enough to be forced into recognizing the
failure of their self-serving endeavors. In these cases, one might
speculate that they did not strive hard enough. Since they never
became completely dedicated to the seeking of their ideal, they
neither reached a point of crisis where a voluntary decision to end
seeking seemed appropriate, nor the point where an involuntary
giving up and reintegration would occur, despite their resistance.

In fact, the majority of ambivalent seekers spend most of their time avoiding the problems that motivate compulsive seeking, and in this way avoid the compensatory seeking of perfection or transcendence. Instead of seeking, one indulges in various diversions, placebos, and escapism.[3] One reads a novel or watches a movie about a heroic seeker, or buys a product associated with a celebrity who corresponds to one's ideal of self-realization. One becomes a voyeur, watching others act out one's own ideals in various media, such as watching television, sports, and reading about success stories in the news. The seeking of the self in this way is delayed, subverted, and avoided, and the tension and conflict necessary for the problem of seeking to be recognized and resolved is never sufficiently aroused.

Indulging in fantasies of heroic quests, diverted by the demands of work, relationships, recreation, drugs and medications, and distracted by the many other demands of living in modern society, serious seeking is put off until later. Since, in this manner, most modern individuals never allow significant suffering from serious seeking to occur, they are never really forced to confront the futility and self-destructiveness of this process. They suffer, but not enough to question their ambivalent identity as a seeker; nor do they suffer enough to force the futility of seeking to the point of resignation and involuntary reintegration.

Paradoxically, this is why only serious seekers who flagrantly tear themselves apart time and again are those who experience reintegration. Apparently, they force the issue to the point where the only alternative to self-destruction—that is, reintegration—seems to happen of its own accord. The distinction between serious and ambivalent seekers is therefore important toward understanding the consequences and outcomes of seeking. It is also important to distinguish the different types of seeking available to the modern self.

The Four Types of Seeking

There are now four general prescriptions for positive change: seeking transcendence; self-realization; self-fulfillment; and self-transformation.

• *Transcendence*

Traditionally, transcendence has been described within the Western tradition as salvation or grace, while in Eastern traditions it has been described as enlightenment—a state in which the desires and concerns of the self and the world lose their power of domination over the individual. Transcendence means that the achieved goal seems final, even though it may be short-lived, because it removes any further need of self-interested seeking. It represents achieving a superior state of consciousness in a vertical ascension above and beyond, at least for a time, independent of the psychological context of the seeking self. Unlike the "descent" and feeling of groundedness that is characteristic of reintegration, transcendence is more of an escape upward into an alternative consciousness than the rediscovery and transformation of an existing form of consciousness.

• *Self-Realization*

Self-realization includes all of the esoteric and mundane disciplines for self-improvement, from psychoanalysis to self-help prescriptions. Self-realization is not oriented toward transcendence, but toward achieving an ideal state of being and functioning in and by the standards of this world. Self-realization does not usually result in an end to seeking, which will often continue in altered form from one goal to the next with no final end. While perfection of the self is the ultimate goal of self-realization, there are endless stages and plateaus to be achieved on the way to this elusive goal. Perfection is never finally achieved, but only more closely approximated, as seeking is endlessly renewed and the goal of perfection is endlessly reformulated.

• *Self-Fulfillment*

Self-fulfillment is the more ordinary and pragmatic accumulation of knowledge, positive recognition, and wealth that has become the predominant form of seeking in modern Western democracies. Although the problems associated with seeking self-fulfillment are not addressed in this book, these problems are often very similar to those associated with other forms of seeking.

is not clearly distinguished from the nonseeking that the author is advocating

• *Self-Transformation*

Self-transformation refers to the reintegration of all of those parts of the psyche that have become dissociated, split off, or repressed from consciousness, and is experienced as a "regrounding." Complete reintegration or self-transformation implies a unitary state of consciousness fundamentally different from, and opposed to, the divisive psychological context of the seeking self. Following self-transformation, identity is contained in and experienced through the body, which is now perceived as an open vessel in communion with the world. This vessel relates through the imagination of embodiment and the perspective of the other (as in animism), rather than through egocentric analysis. Subjectivity tends to be relocated to some degree in the body as opposed to the head, for example in the regions of the heart and abdomen.

The experience of an integrative grounding of consciousness indicates that—unlike Eastern descriptions of transcendence as a movement upward and out through the head—Westerners experience integration as a downward movement of subjectivity and awareness from head to heart to navel or abdomen, and then out into the world. It is this downward movement, a reincorporation of the psyche occurs that is crucial preparation for the Western experience of "soul" and "spirituality." But paradoxically, experiences of reintegration are often misunderstood as a form of transcendence or even of self-realization.

It is likely that much of the literature on the goals and experience of transcendence (the search for grace and enlightenment) and self-realization is actually based on integrative experiences that are misrepresented in terms of the language used to describe these other goals. This confusion results because the current literature on transcendence and self-realization often does not distinguish between any of the above goals. This is especially true of the self-help literature, where metaphors for all types of goals and prescriptions for their attainment are mixed in an eclectic brew of idealisms. For any particular individual, there are likely to be multiple goals and no clear distinctions between them, all of them muddled together in a general desire and search for the good life and the avoidance of suffering.

Seeking and the Postponement of Fulfillment

The average person not only works long hours but sometimes has extra jobs or is getting extra training. Husbands and wives both work. In this process, the present is sacrificed for future well-being—such as promotions, vacations, and retirement—or for the sake of the children, who are also in full-time training for the future. Behind all this lurks a desire to obtain sudden fame, wealth, or to rise above it all in some spiritual transformation of consciousness. But self-sacrifice for future benefit—for the sake of a future reward or idealistic outcome—is nearly always a futile attempt to manipulate fate. The money may be there, but the person who saved it will not be.

In contrast to this frenetic way of life, all individuals ultimately wish to rest in peace, that is, accomplish their goals and enjoy the fruits of their labor—now, not in an afterlife—through unhindered recreation and communion. But once habituated to seeking, it is nearly impossible to abstain from it. If forced to do so, meaning and vitality dissipate, and even death may soon follow. For example, many individuals work all of their lives, looking forward to a happy retirement. But since their entire lives have been defined soley by work and their careers, when retirement actually arrives, their inner reason for being evaporates. In such cases, a premature death often follows. Yet there are no alternatives to seeking because modern Western culture is blindly obsessed with promoting only one point of view. Even if they are lucky enough to have obtained wealth and recognition, individuals cannot enjoy them because they are too busy seeking something else, such as spirituality. Even recreation becomes work, a predetermined schedule of anticlimactic activities.

All modern Western individuals are conditioned from childhood to become seekers in one or more of the four ways previously described, primarily in terms of seeking self-fulfillment. But the other goals are included to spice up the message and ensure engagement. Each individual seeks in a different way, and each has a threshold where seeking becomes a problem and needs to be objectively evaluated and questioned. Not everyone reaches this threshold, but for those who do, a reassessment is in order. How much should be sacrificed of the current self—by saving money, by working harder, by a disciplined preparation for future possibilities, by moralistic striving to become good and spiritual—for the sake of a future self?

There seems to be a cultural consensus in Western democracies that the more seeking and self-sacrifice the better, as if there were something inherently good and even heroic about investing in one's future state of being and providing for future relaxation and enjoyment. These investments tend to be evaluated as a kind of heroic moral strength that comes from striving, self-sacrifice, and, of course, suffering. The same is true for spiritual seeking. Going to church often and regularly, long hours of prayer and meditation, and other spiritual practices, are often seen as preparation for a future state of grace or enlightenment. They are credited as the cause of any attainment that occurs, and provoke the admiration and envy of others who are less disciplined.

In what follows, I question this point of view, and suggest that these attainments would have occurred, perhaps even sooner, without self-sacrifice and seeking—or that they have occurred despite seeking, rather than as a result of it.

Self-sacrifice in the present for future reward, especially in the history of Christianity, is not new, but has a particular saliency and urgency in the modern era. In becoming civilized, modern individuals have been conditioned to delay gratification, but for some this delay continues past retirement until death. Like self-sacrifice, goal seeking also requires the delay of enjoyment. As a result, most learn how to delay, but few learn to spontaneously enjoy in the moment. Recreation begins to resemble work, and forced retirement results in depression and an early death, rather than enjoyment of the fruits of one's labor.

Seeking self-realization or transcendence is a sacrifice of the current self for an imaginary future self, depriving the current self of pleasure, relaxation, and the natural flow of life. Natural experience is foreclosed by the necessity of the concentration, effort, and activity of seeking, even if it is only a vague fantasy with which the self is preoccupied. Seeking results in an unending and ultimately imperfect and even foolish performance upon a stage, critically observed by a godlike tyrannical conscience, society, and ghosts from one's past.

The illusory choice the seeker makes is to sacrifice the quality of life now in the hope that the future quality of life will be substantially improved from what it would have been without this sacrifice. Individuals give up what they have now for something they imagine or wish to be better in the future.

Why should an individual do this? This style of life is, for example, rationalized as necessary for the maintenance of civilization and law and order. We are taught that individuals must be willing to delay gratification and sacrifice present satisfaction for future enjoyment and achievement. But regardless of this and many other suspect reasons justifying this behavior, self-sacrificial seeking is nearly always overdone to the point that it becomes counterproductive. Many civilizations based on this kind of self-sacrifice have come and gone, yet never achieved the utopias their leaders promised, and for which successive generations of workers diligently sacrificed their lives.

The question always arises, How much is enough?—and further, How much is too much? Like the early Christians, modern individuals always hope that utopia is just around the corner, and that they will fairly soon enjoy the benefits of their self-sacrifice, rather than passing on these benefits to some future person for whom they have ceased to exist. But this utopia—the miracle of science that will save modern individuals from death, return expended youth and vitality, and result in freedom from labor and self-sacrifice—is no more than an illusion or wishful thinking. More often than not, self-sacrifice is nothing less than seeking an illusion and failing to learn, or learning too late, that what the individual hoped to find was always there, but was ignored due to self-interested preoccupations.

For seeking to become a problem, it is not necessary that one actually take up a discipline, learn a new vocabulary and theory, or even know very clearly what goal is sought. It is only necessary to have a generic, conditioned belief and faith in such goals. This criterion is always already met in most Western individuals by virtue of social influence, modern education, and exposure to various media, where these goals are "sold" to "consumers" of ideals—attached, of course, to a product, service, celebrity, or traditional authority.

It is not external, social behavior, but the internal psychological preoccupation with the goal of transcendence or self-realization that distinguishes those for whom seeking becomes a problem. A psychological preoccupation with fantasies of self-realization or transcendence, to the point of distraction and internal conflict, is the defining feature of suffering seekers.

This perspective can only make sense to experienced seekers who have learned something about the difficulties and frustrations of seeking. For serious, experienced seekers, the question becomes whether there is freedom of choice about whether to seek, or whether the individual has become an unwilling slave to ideals, destined to sacrifice a lifetime for the sake of an illusion rather than living in the present. It is therefore suggested that seeking, and self-sacrifice in the process of seeking, should be questioned. The actual questions are simple: Is it working?, How is it working?, and How much is enough? Also, What about accepting the self as it is, things as they are, and enjoying life for what it is worth now?

Modern individuals already have an artificial, arbitrary date for the end of seeking—retirement. But by then it is too late to recover what has been sacrificed: namely, youth and the life that has already been expended. The invention of retirement is a symptom of what is wrong with the modern era—the lie that present work is a virtuous sacrifice that will end in reward at the end of life.

Split-Off Identities

As a therapist I have seen many forms of mental illness, but all too often discovered that lurking behind the specific symptoms and complaints was some variation of the general problem of seeking. For example, I was seeing a young woman inmate in therapy in federal prison who heard critical voices that disturbed and distracted her. One of these voices was that of her sexually abusive father, who was constantly telling her what an evil person she was.

Jane, a twenty-two year old single woman, was arrested in a major drug bust, and had several bad experiences on drugs. She had bizarre, fantastic stories to tell about her memories of sexual abuse and of the incidents that led to her arrest. She often approached others hoping to confirm or deny what her internal voices were saying to her, and to support her belief that some of these voices came from other inmates and correctional personnel. The result was that she was rejected and ridiculed by her peers.

Jane had split-off identities that had become independent and hostile to her. These hostile voices, which I will refer to collectively as her *shadow-identity*, haunted her because of her frantic, panic-stricken, and avoidant seeking in response to early traumas.

Seeking had caused those parts of her self that made up the shadow-identity to be split off from and polarized in opposition to her seeking self. These parts were rejected because they were judged to be inferior or obstructive to her overriding goal of seeking to master the original and subsequent traumas. But these split-off part-selves were now mirroring the conscience that had rejected them, and demanding her attention in hope of reincorporation.

Jane's symptoms were therefore complicated and worsened by her seeking to cure herself of them. The symptoms caused by her seeking replaced those that had resulted directly from her original traumas, and these secondary symptoms goaded her to seek even more desperately. Eventually, becoming possessed and obsessed by seeking, she literally became psychologically and physically imprisoned as a result of her ceaseless striving.

The other identity in this internal drama, the guardian of her inner prison, was her *taskmaster conscience* that provoked, criticized, and wounded her like a burr under the yoke of a beast of burden, driving her to run off in every direction away from herself. Losing herself at every turn, she was goaded by her conscience to blindly search for herself everywhere but where she was, in her present experience.

In therapy Jane was seeking to understand what was happening to her, what was wrong, and how to cope with the critical voices. She was so preoccupied with this agenda that she could not live her life, be herself, or relax and enjoy the moment. Having, so to speak, lost her soul—and having become even more lost in searching for her soul—she had understandably panicked, not realizing that her frantic seeking was what continued to prevent the reunification of her soul with her body.

Her incestuous fantasies, whether or not rooted in actual abuse, also symbolized a compensatory fantasy of fusion of the disparate parts of her psyche that she was striving so hard to keep estranged. The horror of losing control, of being taken over by an hostile identity (those part-selves seeking to reunite with her), and losing her remaining sense of identity (based on her seeking), goaded her into a panic-stricken battle for survival. In this battle, she was obsessed with fending off attempts by these disparate and hostile part-selves that were trying to break down her resistance—what remained of her identity—and re-unite with her psyche as a whole.

In therapy, I focused on accepting her as she was, listening to her, and leaving her alone. I carefully avoided any therapeutic problem-solving or prescriptions, while acknowledging the importance of the concerns she brought to therapy. By avoiding the roles of critic, prescriber, or obstructer of her agenda for change—and most importantly, by just being there for her as a person she could trust and depend upon—I helped her to calm down, to slow her frantic attempts to understand, and to relax her blind groping to regain contact with herself. In therapy, I neither rejected nor scolded her resistance to reintegration, which was manifested as seeking; and I was regularly available to her, so that she could begin to slough off onto me some of the great responsibility she felt toward herself, which was also manifested in seeking. Because of increased self-acceptance, Jane was given an opportunity to relax, to recognize that her crisis was not as acute as she had thought, and to become conscious of herself as a tolerable human being.

After a few months she snapped out of it, as if relaxing after a panic attack. She had come down to earth, reinhabiting her body. Suddenly, Jane was focusing on her outer world and speaking to people, rather than listening to internal voices and getting caught up in bad memories. I attribute her recovery in part to being able to sit with someone who did not judge her or have any expectations of her, with whom she could eventually ground herself and begin to see herself for what she was, in her own way and on her own schedule. To whatever degree I was able to provide a benign substitute for her sadomasochistic conscience, to that degree she was relieved of the pathology of seeking.

Many seekers have symptoms like hers, a paranoid concern with the assumed, projected critical thoughts and expectations of others toward them, and a frantic need to do something about these critical thoughts and unrealistic expectations. They become "empty strivers," seeking to fill the same void that was created by their flight from their original self. This can easily become a form of self-enslavement and madness. But in order to bring an end to empty striving, the desperate need for a solution—for something real with which to fill the void—must first be greatly reduced or entirely removed. This desperate need for a solution, however, cannot be removed through seeking, but only through its exhaustion or relaxation.

Trusting Relationship

One ancient style of coping with empty-striving through relaxation rather than exhaustion is faith or trust. This type of faith is not necessarily a religious belief in God, but faith in the sense that recognizing and accepting one's fate has always been one's only, and best, option. This requires a discipline of waiting to see what will happen, a conscious avoidance of premature seeking to alter outcomes, and trust that the outcome of events and one's place in them will be as it ought to be. This trust may eventually be fully realized in the form of loving one's fate, an outcome that always accompanies integrative experiences.

Children provide a good example of how faith or trust works. It is only to the extent that children trust and have faith in their parents that they can be children, rather than young adults. Similarly, it is only when adults can somehow trust themselves, others, the world, and their place in it, that they can stop meddling with fate and relax their guard in order to openly participate in and enjoy life as it is. To do anything else constitutes a tragic refusal to live the only life one can live.

The universal prehistoric religion of ancestor worship was based upon trust of former and subsequent generations of family members, and in the integrity and continuity of the current family. Male heads of the household, responsible for the sustenance and worship of their forefathers, were guaranteed similar sustenance and worship in the afterlife by surviving family members. Provided the family remained intact and faithful to blood ties and custom, nothing short of a disaster could interfere with a happy and blissful afterlife. Consequently, striving was inappropriate and had no place beyond fulfilling one's duties in this worship.[4]

It is possible to understand the function of Christianity in a similar way, as offering the opportunity to experience faith—in God, Jesus Christ, or Providence—for the purpose of curing individuals from a false belief in their total responsiblity for their circumstances and fate. Christian doctrines that support this perspective include the Atonement, in which Jesus Christ sacrificed himself to save all subsequent human beings from the necessity of suffering and of earning penitence from original sin; this reassured Christians that they were, in effect, already saved. The doctrine of providence, like the earlier concept of fate that preceded it, suggested that everything had been determined already; therefore, nothing need be done about it. The sacraments provided immediate reassurance of one's status as saved. Even the idea of original sin supported this point of view, by teaching that all spiritual striving must be based on prideful motives; therefore, it was sinful to seek spirituality, and nothing useful could be done to alter one's fate. Finally, the later Protestant doctrine of justification by faith summed up this point of view:

According to Martin Luther, faith was the key to a relationship with a gracious God, the One who loved and gave grace. With the initiative in God's hands, the individual was free to serve and love self and others. This paradoxical liberation through dependence was due to the realization of freedom from striving.[5]

For Martin Luther, faith liberated the self from servitude to self-interest and the preoccupation with uneasiness that came from a lack of self-acceptance.

Eastern philosophies and religions have similar points of view. For example, according to Shinran (1173–1263 C.E.), the Buddha Amida's vow to save all human beings had already been accomplished. Since all "ways of effort" were therefore useless, the Buddhist need only rely on "the power of the other." In his "Song of the Nembutsu," Shinran summarized this perspective as follows:

The ceaseless, boundless immeasurable
    activity of Namu Amida Butsu [his
    Vow to save all beings]
Awakens me to what is real and true.
This is my reliance,
My refuge,
My wholehearted trust . . .
Just as I am,
This all-embracing Vow enables me to
    become a Buddha! . . .
When we once entrust to the vessel of
    Amida's Vow— . . .

Our birth in the Pure Land is assured! . . .
At the very moment of our entrusting . . .
We are enabled to see the truth of
    things-as-they-are,
Of suchness,
So that we instantaneously become an
    avenue
For the wisdom and compassion of the
    Buddha.
. . . when we ordinary foolish beings
Realize the mind of true entrusting, . . .
Though we still wander in samsara:
    the world of birth and death,
At this same time we are shown Nirvana:
    the world of the Buddha . . .[6]

This kind of trusting relationship must have been central in many student/teacher relationships in all religions, from past to present. Sometimes this type of faith, trust, or dependence upon another can be reproduced for a time in a therapeutic relationship where it may be referred to as a "positive transference." The client in this relationship may hand over responsibility for watching over and guiding the self to the therapist. This allows the therapist to act as a positive conscience, and temporarily frees the client from the conflictual dynamics of the seeking self. This provides the client with a glimpse of the state of mind that may eventually result from the successful treatment of the seeking self, in which peace of mind is attained and the critical, taskmaster conscience is dissolved.

Dedicated seekers, often for good reasons, have stopped relying on others to support this dependent function, beginning with separation from parents, then friends, and then lovers and spouses. Therapy has become commonplace in the twentieth century precisely because Western individualism and secularism has isolated individuals from opportunities to depend upon others and nature in general. At a certain threshold, this isolation and increased sense of responsibility drives some individuals to seek self-realization, so that all will love him or her, or to transcendence, so that loving relationships will no longer be needed.

As long as Jane continued seeking, her symptoms remained. But once she stopped seeking, the symptoms disappeared, and she was able to speak with one voice. In her experience and in many other cases, seeking had become the primary symptom; seeking replaced the original disorder, which was now only a symbolic memory of abuse and loss in the distant past. In cases like hers, to search for an original cause, and a cure of that cause, would be to avoid the more important recognition of the current cause of her suffering—the self-destructive and futile conflict that resulted from her seeking.

Once she had, so to speak, woken up from her bad dream, Jane was no longer dependent upon her therapist. I had helped to provide the vehicle for her rescue, but she could now trust herself and occasionally others within limits, and no longer needed therapy. The crucial point is that a trusting relationship provided the vehicle for reintegration. This sense of trust allowed Jane to relax her compulsive seeking and helped her to trust herself. After this the vehicle could be discarded, because her more integrated psyche was better able to relax and care for itself.

* * *

Tom, a twenty-one year old pizza deliverer, was referred to me for outpatient treatment by his parents because he had made suicidal statements. His suicidal feelings were the result of his failure to perform successfully in professional baseball tryouts for the minor leagues. Tom had been fairly successful in a local league, and a recruiter to whom he had written expressed some interest, but nothing resulted from his search for recognition.

Tom lived at home and threatened to quit his job because it was degrading to his self-image, and because it provided inadequate income for independent living. Tom was only willing to live as a professional baseball player, but he was rapidly approaching an age when he would be too old to be accepted. He went to several professional team tryouts, but always did poorly. He was too slow running bases and couldn't hit the pitches or throw the ball all the way to home plate from the outfield.

Tom reached a turning point when I mentioned I had waited twenty years before achieving my own professional goals. Over time he began to accept the fact that it need not be life-threatening for him to fail to achieve a particular ideal. Tom's problem was not only his difficulties in seeking a specific goal, but also his tendency to choose unrealistic ideal goals, and his all-or-nothing thinking. He believed that he must succeed in baseball or life would not be worth living.

Tom did not achieve his goal of becoming a professional baseball player, nor did he commit suicide. Instead, he came to realize during therapy that there were many alternatives; that life could be lived without achieving ideal goals, and that he had plenty of time to decide how he wanted to live.

Origins of the Seeking Self

Finally! Of course, much seeking is realistic, useful, even necessary, and does not result in mental illness. But seeking that is a reaction to significant problems may foster even more significant problems. Seeking is usually a response to a feeling of lack or psychological pain. In psychological terms, this pain is referred to as a narcissistic wound, based on the shocking discovery that one is not loved by everyone, or not by the right persons. This sense of inadequacy produces an urgent personal need to heal the wound.

At bottom, underneath all of the successive layers concealing vulnerability, shame, and fear of rejection, these unfulfilled needs are anchored in the desire to be loved unconditionally, by self and others, for what one is. The response of seeking to fill this need may either be helpful, by dealing directly with the specific problem at hand, or obstructive, by an avoidant and futile seeking elsewhere. Seeking becomes obstructive when it involves searching for a remote and unrealistic solution, for example, seeking extraordinary accomplishment, radical self-improvement, or celebrity status in order to win the love of everyone.

In this way, seeking often becomes a form of avoidance. But if the original problem of unlovability or intolerance of one's imperfections by others is avoided by pursuing a transcendent state of being or ideal self, the original problem is ignored and aggravated. Yet, should the original problem be aggravated, it may swell in importance and power, and further drive an individual to flee from one's present life through dedication to an illusory future of ideal, untroubled existence.

To the extent an individual seeks a solution in a future goal rather than facing the present situation—for example, recognizing and mourning the loss of one's idealistic fantasies—the original problem becomes the forgotten and irrelevant cause of the distorted, psychological dynamics that are the driving force behind seeking. A splitting of the self occurs as it is driven to self-denial and distracted from living. Instead of being present, the self becomes preoccupied with illusions and stratagems to find release from empty striving and suffering, but never faces the actual source of its suffering. The unlovable self begins to feel like a slave driven by unseen, unacknowledged powers, which it is. On the one hand, it is driven by a shadow-identity it refuses to acknowledge. On the other hand, it is driven by a judgmental, perfectionistic, taskmaster conscience to which it must continually submit with endless performances.

In extreme cases, the shadow-identity and judgmental conscience may become an internal voice or voices, criticizing the self to the point of distraction, and eventually driving the individual into madness. In milder cases, the shadow-identity and bad conscience only show up in dreams, usually in embarrassing, foolish behaviors and mistakes of the dreamer; in nightmarish, hostile encounters with monstrous dream characters; or perhaps as a hostile rival who always obtains the love and admiration of others.

For the shadow-identity to be reintegrated and the tyrannical conscience and its ideals dethroned, they must be faced. The seeking behaviors that are the vehicle of dominance of the shadow-identity and the conscience over the self must be given up. If seeking is not given up, the self will continue to be driven by a bad conscience that, by its nature, avoids the acknowledgment and reintegration of the opposing shadow-identity. This opposing shadow-identity consists of those parts of the self that have been split off and rejected because they seemed incompatible with the future, ideal goals of the seeking self. Rather than forming a cohesive identity, these part-selves are only loosely associated by their common fate and opposition to the seeking self.

Provoked by rejection, the part-selves of the shadow-identity lash back and intrude into consciousness; they disrupt and divert the self from heroic performance in its quest for perfection. This in turn enrages the conscience. Once this standoff has been established, internal conflict becomes a way of life, foreclosing any potential for experiencing an integrated psyche in communion with others and the world. Life and the love of living are disregarded by the harried seeker, who has now become preoccupied with a quest, based on the ultimately futile hope that the self can save itself from itself.

Summary

The points made in this chapter are as follows:

1. Seeking is a reaction to discontent and disillusionment, and ultimately to a lack of trust in and love of one's fate and of one's self.

2. There are four types of seeking: seeking transcendence (salvation, enlightenment, or grace); self-realization; self-fulfillment; and self-transformation or integration.

3. Disciplines for seeking transcendence and self-realization are misleading and unlikely to produce as advertised. Self-transformation can only occur when these disciplines fail, are given up, or relaxed, voluntarily or involuntarily.

4. Seeking that is preoccupied with the self and with future idealistic goals for the self will lead to the splitting off of a separate shadow-identity which consists of rejected part-selves opposed to seeking, and a negative, judgmental conscience, which creates and enforces endless self-improvement agendas.

Wisdom Sample 2

S IMILAR WAYS of understanding the problem of striving were developed in ancient India and China, complementing each other in their emphasis on *disinterested action* and *effortless activity*. The *Bhagavad Gita* is an Indian book about a war that occurred sometime between 1400 and 800 B.C.E. This book was put in writing between 400 B.C.E. and 200 C.E., but existed as an oral tradition long before this. The *Gita* contains a dialogue between Arjuna and Krishna, the latter representing the god Vishnu.

One of the chief lessons Krishna has to offer Arjuna is that disinterested action leads to transcendence, called Brahma. Disinterested action is characterized by a lack of self-concern about the fruits of one's actions. This ideal of action without attachment is repeatedly referred to by Krishna, who calls himself the *eternal nondoer*. It is not actions that are to be avoided, only the self-interested desire that binds one to them.

Krishna states that the way of nonaction is obscure; he counsels against hope, envy, and possessiveness, and advocates impartiality to success and failure. In the following quote, Krishna summarizes his views on action and nonaction:

> I desire no fruit of actions,
> and actions do not defile me; . . .
> The wise say a man is learned
> when his plans lack constructs
>   of desire,
> when his actions are burned
> by the fire of knowledge.

Abandoning attachment to fruits
of action, always content,
    independent,
he does nothing at all
even when he engages in action.
He incurs no guilt if he has
    no hope,
restrains his thought and himself,
abandons possessions,
and performs actions with his
    body only.
Content with whatever comes by
    chance,
beyond dualities, free from envy,
impartial to failure and success,
he is not bound even when he acts.[7]

A similar point of view became the basis for the ancient Chinese philosophy of Taoism. According to Lao Tzu, a legendary old master who may have lived around 600 B.C.E., even before the development of agriculture, society and mental health had begun to deteriorate. At first "there was a dawning of deliberate effort, everyone was on the verge of leaving their innocent mind and . . . their virtues were complex and not unified."[8] This was followed by the legend of Huang Ti, believed to have lived in the twenty-seventh century B.C.E., whose story "represents the subordination of earthly dominion to the quest for freedom and perfection of the spirit."[9] Following this, however, in the times of the Shang-Yin dynasty people came to relish and desire things, and intelligence was seduced by externals. Essential life lost its reality.[10]

Finally, the fall of humankind was completed in the Chou dynasty, when the point was reached where "everyone wants to employ knowledge and craft for recognition in society and loses the basis of the overall source."[11]

Addressing this deteriorated condition, Lao Tzu recommended that the best way to act and think is *wu-wei*, effortless activity. Wu-wei does not mean non-action, but action without friction or contention; wu-wei refers to action without ulterior motives of gain or loss, praise or blame, reward or punishment. The most efficient "way" to overcome problems or adversity is by non-contention or yielding, which is not submission or capitulation, but taking the "way" of least resistance. Power and virtue cannot be strived for, but emerge naturally.

Rather than develop sophistication, erudition, or cunning, one should return to infancy. The "way" or *tao* refers to the way things do what they do, an effortless, natural performance:

The sage
    dwells in affairs of nonaction,
carries out a doctrine without words.
He lets the myriad creatures rise up
    but does not instigate them;
He acts
    but does not presume;

He completes his work
>
> but does not dwell on it.[12]

For Lao Tzu, values always proved self-defeating. Pursuing a moral ideal did not make one moral, but resulted in one who acted morally in a calculating and deliberate fashion, rather than naturally and spontaneously. Holding ideals in high esteem resulted in conflict. Since ideals required striving, they separated those who were above from those below on the ladder of valuation, consequently encouraging those below to try and overthrow those who looked down on them from above. The "way" taught that cumulative moral learning was counterproductive to living naturally:

Who acts fails;

Who grasps loses.

For this reason,

>
> The sage does not act.

Therefore,

>
> He does not fail.

>
> He does not grasp.

Therefore,

>
> He does not lose.[13]

* * *

Who is puffed up cannot stand,

Who is self-absorbed has no distinction,

Who is self-revealing does not shine,

Who is self-assertive has no merit,

Who is self-praising does not last long.

As for the Way, we may say these are

"excess provisions and excess baggage."

Creation abhors such extravagances.

Therefore,

One who aspires to the Way,

does not abide in them.[14]

Chapter 2

The Shadow-Identity

THE SHADOW-IDENTITY consists of those parts of the self unacceptable to the seeker: the wish to be taken care of; rebellion against goal-seeking agendas; realizations of powerlessness and futility in the goal-seeking process; childish tendencies to play, to be irresponsible, and engage in the spontaneous, creative exploration of rule-breaking; and other desires and attributes incompatible with the seeking self. These attributes threaten the perceived lovability of the self, as seen through the "tough love" of a bad and controlling conscience. The shadow-identity is the collective enemy of the seeker, disrupting, obstructing, and contradicting the pursuit of the seeker's agendas. This concept of the shadow-identity is partly inspired by Carl Jung's description of the "shadow,"[1] but has significant differences in emphasis. The shadow-identity is rarely a distinct identity, and this term is used here to refer to those aspects of the unconscious constellated in opposition to the seeking self.

The more the seeking self, dominated by a tyrannical, taskmaster conscience, is threatened by its enemy, the shadow-identity, the more forcefully the conscience attempts to maintain its control over the self. In responding to the overzealous conscience, the more passionately the seeking self strives, the more it must sacrifice of itself, in part through the rejection of those parts of itself that seem to interfere with the quest. The more that is sacrificed to the idol of the ideal, the stronger the shadow-identity becomes, as more and more unacceptable impulses and traits are revealed and rejected by the increasingly perfectionistic conscience. These rejected impulses and traits, which are authentic parts of the personality, by default become members of the growing collective opposition of the shadow-identity.

The Divided Personality

From its origins in a unified psyche, seeking creates an internalized "three-person psychology." These three parts are:

1) A *conscience* identified with abstract ideals, which it continually imposes on the self as goals. Because the conscience continually imposes goals on the self, it often becomes a taskmaster, or *taskmaster conscience*.

2) An unlovable *self*, whose only redemption from complete rejection by an overscrupulous conscience is through constant performance in seeking or imitating the ideals of the conscience. This is the seeking self.

3) An opposing collective *shadow-identity*, whose part-selves intrusively attempt to remind the self of the need to reintegrate those parts of the psyche the conscience has forced the self to reject and repress.

Partly as a result of the interventions of the shadow-identity which embarrass the seeking self and provoke the conscience, the more a person strives for transcendence or self-realization, the more that person's behavior appears to others as distracted, self-centered, and foolish. In order to compensate for the one-sided attitudes of the personality, both the shadow-identity and others will make fun of the seeker, try to trip her up, try to get her to take it easy, have some fun, and laugh a little. This opposition comes from those parts of the self that have been rejected and desire recognition and reintegration now. It also comes from those people who feel rejected and want a relationship *now*, and not in some nonexistent, utopian future.

The internal opposition of the shadow-identity shows up in conflictual dreams, in embarrassing mistakes, in strong desires that raise questions about one's commitments, in laziness, isolation, feelings of inferiority and unworthiness, forgetting, and in comically poor performance. The internal conflict created by seeking is further exacerbated by the increasing performance demands of the conscience due to lack of attainment. Internal conflict also originates from unconscious resentments that arise in the self. On the one hand, the self feels deprived due to the excessive sacrifices it has made in order to become worthy and loved. On the other hand, due to the sacrifices it has made in pursuit of an ideal, the self feels deprived of the opportunities it has lost in which to enjoy the common pleasures of living.

As the seeking self narrows its horizons and becomes increasingly distracted from natural experience by its preoccupation with seeking, the shadow-identity becomes more powerful. The two poles—the rebellious shadow-identity and the model of the ideal self imposed by the taskmaster conscience—move farther apart as they continue to separate into conflicting opposites. The striving self pursues an ever more remote and transcendent ideal, while the shadow-identity becomes ever more wishful, infantile, intrusive, and obstructive. Instead of progress toward integration, there is increasing disintegration as the gulf between self and ideal widens, and the incompatibility between the warring poles of the psyche becomes more pronounced.

Another aspect of the shadow-identity is that of a radically uncivilized and unpredictable free spirit. This aspect is more flexible and expressive than the self, because of its lack of constraints and inhibitions. Western media are not only in love with ideal goals and individuals, but also with shadow-figures that appear in films as successful criminals, Don Juan-type lovers, anarchic revolutionaries, and amoral, hostile characters such as old-West gunfighters who take what they want rather than earn it. They are the illegitimate third person who inspires jealousy, because they attract the interest and admiration of one's friends and lovers and seem capable of anything they choose to pursue. The shadow-identity usurps one's place as the center of attention and love in the world, threatening to leave one abandoned and without support. To the extent that this threat is also realized by rivals in one's external relationships, the self is further goaded toward the dedicated seeking of perfection.

It is, finally, the shadow-identity rather than the collective ideal of the conscience that contains the cure—the answer—for the seeker. What has been rejected and denied, when allowed to reintegrate, will provide the self with the balance, grounding in experience, confidence, pleasure, and peace of mind it was mistakenly seeking in the collective ideal.

The splitting of the self into three—the shadow-identity, the seeking self, and the taskmaster conscience imposing the goal of an ideal self—must finally be healed by the reunion of the self and shadow-identity. But this can only occur through the abandonment of the ghost of the ideal self and the refusal to perform for its militant advocate. Integration may then occur by virtue of the absence of the internal conflict and self-hatred that maintained disintegration.

The Ungrounded Self

William, a formerly successful artist, was brought in by his girlfriend to see me for therapy. He had been experiencing suicidal thoughts because of a long period of inability to paint. This was accompanied by depression, some loss of identity, and loss of purpose. After a few months of talking about his lack of creativity, and my attempting to point out that his preoccupation with recovering creativity was the main obstacle to its return, William related the following dream.

He had journeyed by boat across the sea at night. Then, through a narrow gap, his boat entered a bay and landed at a small town. So far, this dream was a classic example of the heroic, spiritual journey, the guiding fantasy of the taskmaster conscience. But after landing, William went to a nightclub, where he was performing music with a guitar for an audience that included his parents, when he noticed that he was naked from the waist down. William felt foolish, but continued to act as if he were a successful entertainer, and as if everything were okay.

I discreetly tried to point out to William that his spiritual striving, according to the demands of the taskmaster conscience, was bringing out the fool or shadow-identity in him; it was exposing him as a fraud, and that he should pay attention to this message. His shadow-identity was rebelling against his obsession with striving after creativity, "em-bare-assing" him, as it were; it was showing him that, instead of being a successful seeker, his striving was a grandstanding performance that only made him more vulnerable, and exposed him to ridicule. His journey had become an imposture, a premature celebration designed to conceal, rather than heal, his disintegration.

As a result of his striving, William had become ungrounded. His "lower half"—his earthly and bodily desires, feelings, and relationships—were dissociated, and were therefore exposing themselves independently in a parody of his soul-searching. As William's dream showed quite elegantly, what he was avoiding in his quest needed reintegration. He needed to come down out of his creative abstractions and vain preoccupations with his former celebrity status and reinhabit his body. He needed once again to become grounded in the world and in his relationships.

Creativity now resided in the fool in William, not in the mind of the serious goal- and performance-oriented adult who sought far and wide for what was already at hand. The shadow-identity showed up as the unconsciously exhibitionistic, embarrassing fool, because that was the part of him that was militantly denied once William had become obsessively engaged in his narrow search for the ideal self whom all would admire and love. The constriction of the search progressively excluded important parts of his unlovable self, which then joined the opposition. Finally, the mind/body split caused by William's seeking was parodied in his dream by exposing his neglected and denied lower half. But while his "lower half" was incompatible with the high-minded celebrity who performed for his parents, it was, in fact, his anchor to the world.

As William's dream shows, the shadow-identity frequently frightens the seeking self and the judgmental conscience with visions of the unlovable parts of the personality that are opposed to the ideal self. In reaction to this threatening vision of imperfection, the mental process of switching attention from the problem to problem-solving occurs almost automatically. But this defensively diverts attention from shameful problem to idealistic cure, from present pain to hope for future bliss. It is so much easier to see one's self as a seeker than as a sufferer; easier to try to erase all relationship problems by becoming a celebrity than to acknowledge specific problems in the present moment.

This premature and automatic transition from a problem to preoccupation with a compensatory goal makes it impossible to come to terms with the difficulties and tragedies of life. The self is habituated by modern culture to respond this way because various forms of seeking are the engine of modern American civilization, which promotes seeking indiscriminately as part of the fundamental right to "life, liberty, and *the pursuit of happiness*." But this pursuit, instead of leading to happiness, for many becomes a prescription for suffering and self-destruction. This suffering is finally and fully realized when retirement fails to even partially compensate for the sacrifice of youth, or failed relationships leave one's ability to trust oneself and others in ruins.

Summary

The points made in this chapter are:

1. If seeking splits the psyche in three, the only worthwhile goal is to become one again. Becoming one means putting an end to the self-serving seeking that created the three selves—conscience, shadow-identity, and seeking self—which compete for dominance in the modern American psyche.

2. Premature problem-solving and goal-seeking is a diversion that forecloses understanding and acceptance. The search for a cure prevents the immediate recognition, reconciliation, and healing that can only occur through facing the problem that provoked the suffering in the first place. Seeking typically diverts attention from the original problem and the necessity of self-acceptance.

Wisdom Sample 3

T HE ancient Greek tragedies often portrayed a struggle between acceptance of what is and the desire for and efforts to attain transcendence. This struggle inevitably resulted in tragic strife and loss. Motivated by exposure to misfortune, humanity's ambition to transcend resulted in further misfortune. The cascade of disaster resulting from inappropriate seeking was the essential plot of many of the early tragic plays in Greece in the sixth and fifth centuries B.C.E.

The tragic conflict over whether or not to attempt to master one's fate is summarized by Martha Nussbaum:

> All humans alike end yoked like animals, whether because of their rage or because of their innocence . . . If you attempt to yoke it [e.g., fate or destiny] you violate and are yoked; if you acknowledge it you melt away.[2]

From the tragic point of view, there was no exit, no freedom, and no progressive, developmental option; the point of Greek tragedy was to illustrate this. But to accept this conclusion left one without hope or a constructive response, causing the individual identity to "melt away." Attempting to control one's destiny had one set of negative consequences and not attempting to control it had another. The sickness of a rage for control was a reaction to a fateful paralysis of will, another kind of sickness. But for the Greeks active acceptance and willing dependence was always preferable to defying the gods.

To seek transcendence was to provoke the envy and wrath of

the gods, who would then punish such seekers as an example for others. Tragedy reinforced this lesson, and provided a forewarning of the tragic fate that has become the inevitable destiny of the modern American self, which seeks to become godlike and determine its destiny.

The Greek solution was a form of self-acceptance, an attitude with similarities to other contemporary perspectives in India (the *Bhagavad Gita*) and China (the Taoism of Lao Tzu). For example, in Sophocles' tragic play *Antigone*, Tiresias, a priest of Apollo, counsels that good thinking is associated with "yielding"—flexibility and renounciation of self-willed stubbornness. Practical wisdom required going with the flow of things and remaining open to the influence of fate, luck, and other uncontrolled forces. To deny or attempt to control these forces was to ensure a tragic outcome. Like the contemporary Eastern solutions, early Greek tragedy seems to suggest a voluntary approach to reintegration by warning, through dramatic examples, of the consequences of impious seeking.

Following an early preoccupation with the tragedy of the heroic seeker, Greek playwrights began to explore tragicomedy in which the role of the fool was emphasized to balance out the seriousness and one-sidedness of the hero. This signaled the beginning of a transition from a religious understanding toward a more psychological understanding of the problem of seeking. Instead of provoking jealous gods, the hero set himself up as a fool to be exposed by the laughter of the audience, a response that helped to offset fear of rejection and also helped to relieve the audience from its own tragicomic suffering.

Chapter 3

The Paradox of Seeking

A NY INVOLVEMENT of the self in striving will be futile as long as the goal of striving is a fundamental change in the self. It is impossible to try to change the self without critical self-evaluation. But this critical attitude must include an element of self-hate and a corresponding degree of internal division and conflict. Paradoxically, though the self cannot transform itself, it may be involuntarily transformed if it gives up all self-judgment and the underlying quest for self-improvement.

Unfortunately, there are few meaningful secular models for giving up striving apart from play, recreation, and retirement. Nevertheless, these options provide important clues about what is being sought—freedom from the constraints of seeking itself. The seriousness of seeking, the self-concern focused on improving the self, create a straitjacket that makes it impossible to explore and enjoy life as it is with its inevitable limitations. Having imprisoned oneself within these constraints, and having suffered rather than benefited from them, there is only one thing to do—break out of them. But how to do this, and where to go? These questions are themselves fundamentally flawed from the point of view of experiencing reintegration. Confusion between means and goals, and the tendency to act out one's anxiety in a premature quest, are some of the inevitable consequences of being brought up in a culture that is habituated to seeking.

Even for those who become addicted to idealisms, there is generally some confusion about goals and the means to achieve them. The esoteric goals of self-realization and transcendence are not easily defined, and seekers usually do not know, beyond some flowery language and vague imagery, anything about the specific goals they are actually seeking. They nevertheless exhaust themselves in futile preoccupation with personal and traditional fantasies about their goals and the prescribed methods of realizing them.

Psychological preoccupation with a quest will inevitably result in the individual becoming a slave to the stated and unstated demands of the chosen goal. This is true even if one does little or nothing to comply with the prescribed methods for reaching the goal. Once the self becomes psychologically dependent upon a quest, it is only a matter of time until the futile seeking of the heroically configured self becomes personally embarrassing, and symptoms of internal conflict and unrest become increasingly evident. As defeat looms on the horizon, depression begins to paralyze the seeker, who eventually seems only to be treading water in order to avoid drowning in anonymity or failure.

Alternatives to Seeking

It is relatively easy to become a seeker, having been habituated from birth to do so, but how does one give it up, accept life as it is, and enjoy what can be enjoyed? There are two alternatives, neither as simple as it sounds.

One alternative is to simply stop seeking, to give it up, relax the internal tension and preoccupation, and stop creating internal conflict, indulgence in self-hate, and persistence in self-wrought suffering. It seems likely that before the modern era, religion may have often served this purpose by inculcating faith that current events would either have a good outcome or somehow be justified. But in the modern era, due to prior habituation and ongoing cultural encouragement, for someone to effectively utilize the path of faith and trust, or a voluntary relaxation of seeking, at the very least requires substantial help and support from others.

Unfortunately, constructive counsel toward giving up seeking is not generally available. On the other hand, there is no lack of support, wanted or unwanted, for continued or renewed seeking. Yet without faith or a voluntary relaxation, a natural end of seeking can only occur due to exhaustion from excessive striving.

Another alternative is to learn how *to seek without self-interest*, without creating internal conflict and splitting. This may be even more difficult, and is probably impossible for those seeking self-realization or transcendence. It seems likely that only by means of integration can seeking lose its self-interested distortions and self-destructiveness. If this is the case, then learning to seek without self-interest is not an option for the seeker.

Seeking is so thoroughly habituated in the childhood of modern individuals that it cannot be given up voluntarily. Whether or not it is acted out in actual behavior, it will continue in fantasy, and the self will remain divided and in internal conflict no matter how much one resolves to give up seeking. To frustrate matters further, attempting to give up seeking, or attempting to seek without self-interest, is to risk engaging in another form of seeking with the same consequences. Under these complex and paradoxical circumstances, when a positive outcome occurs, it always seems mysterious and inexplicable, leading many to assume it must be divine intervention.

* * *

Robert, another federal inmate I worked with in therapy, had been a successful contractor. He believed he had been railroaded into prison on a bogus marijuana charge. He was preoccupied with fighting the charges against him and with his relationship to his devoted wife, who had moved nearby so she could visit him. After some time in treatment, Robert suddenly relaxed and felt free of his preoccupation about his concerns. Nothing had changed in terms of his circumstances, but he was suddenly relaxed and comfortable about his situation. Suddenly, he was able to enjoy the limited freedoms and recreations available in the prison setting.

What had changed was how Robert was reacting to his situation, not what he was doing about it. Through this change of attitude, which neither he nor I could explain or even describe, he was more likely to be successful and obtain what he wanted. He was also able to have a life while pursuing his goal, and felt no anxiety about the outcome. This was an example of giving up seeking while still going through the motions, or acting without self-interest." "attachment to outcome"

Robert might easily have suffered intensely for at least several more years had this change not occurred. But evidently, further suffering was not necessary in order for him to change in the way he did. Given a religious outlook, Robert might have interpreted this change as divine intervention. From a secular point of view, he could have interpreted it to be the result of his own seeking or the result of therapy. But having experienced integration, interpretation was not important. He did not know what had happened or how it had happened, and simply went on about the business of his life with an inner, secret sense of liberation.

There are those who say that the achievement of ideal goals requires suffering, and this is no doubt true. But it is also true that there should be a limit to suffering. This limit begins to become evident when the pursuit of healing of the culturally-conditioned rift in the psyche itself becomes the reason for continued suffering. While this rift cannot be avoided in the present Western cultural context, it need not be maintained naively or made worse. Allowing for the conditioned need to follow idealistic pursuits, the voluntary or involuntary giving up of striving, or attachment to the outcome, remains the key to attaining inner peace.

Sometimes this giving up of self-interested seeking means nothing in regard to actual behavior, which continues as before. It may only require giving up the internal obsession and conflict, and the self-interested preoccupations that are byproducts of seeking.

If pursuit of the ideal self leads to the point where the individual experiences integration, there will no longer be any choice in the matter. But as long as the individual has a choice, the pursuit of overly idealistic goals should be recognized as a product of wishful thinking. The romantic and heroic valuation of seeking in our culture is pervasive but misplaced. Instead, to restrain from acting out heroic quests is a demonstration of mature experience and knowledge.

Usually only the most ardent seekers come to recognize the futility of their striving. Among them, only a few experience an involuntary reintegration. This involuntary reintegration can be understood as a stage of maturation, a growing out of the youthful and enthusiastic pursuit of ideals. The youthful stage of ardent self-interested seeking must occur in contemporary American culture, but it must also be outgrown. Modern American culture, idolizing youth, perpetuates this overzealous enthusiasm as if it were the one and only way to live, the normative ideal.

The Paradoxical Quest

Transformation does not occur as a result of striving, but only when the end of the rope has been reached and striving is finally given up. Seeking may finally end through a sudden realization, a change in perspective, or through some type of involuntary release. At this point, reintegration may—or may not—occur spontaneously. The terms *salvation*, *grace*, *enlightenment*, and *transcendence* are sometimes used to refer to the experience of the reunification of split-off portions of the psyche, renewed as a whole, after the mechanism creating their separation and conflict has ceased to operate. This mechanism is the heroic seeker on a quest for self-realization or transcendence. Diametrically opposed to the psychology of the heroic seeker is the transformed, unified, or integrated psyche, which has no need or desire to change itself.

In a paradoxical sense, striving is not only a given, but is necessary. Unity cannot be attained or appreciated until it is preceded by and compared to disunity. Similarly, peace of mind cannot be appreciated unless preceded by and compared with internal conflict. Some degree of inner division always occurs at some point in childhood or adolescence, at which time striving begins to become a way of life. The unity of childhood is then projected onto the adult, and one seeks to become what the next stage of unity is imagined to be, in the form of a powerful, integrated, autonomous, and mature individual. Few, however, fully achieve this positively envisioned self, which tends to recede into idealisms as time goes on.

Despite this necessary preliminary seeking, however, striving is not responsible for, and has no influence on, transformative outcomes. Integration can only begin when self-interested striving ceases, or ceases to matter. Integration can also occur while striving continues, but only if the nature of the striving is altered by the integrative process to remove self-interested attachment to the process and outcome. In this case also, transformation is not a product of striving, but occurs independent of it or, one might even say, despite it.

There is no guarantee that striving will wear itself out or that an integration will occur while it is ongoing; instead, striving generally becomes chronic, repetitive, and futile. This is because the consequences of striving are not understood and because of continuing self-interest in the process. The close association of striving with an ongoing sense of self-worth means that a giving up of striving is experienced as a retreat from the vitality—and even the life—of the self. Because the giving up of striving may be experienced as a psychological death, this explains why it is so difficult to give up seeking, and why it so easily becomes the cause of chronic suffering.

Fear of the death of the self provides a clue as to what the problem with striving is. It is like an addiction or a prop the self believes it cannot do without. And this belief is basically correct. The modern American self and its taskmaster conscience are created by self-serving ethical evaluations—"this is good, this is bad"; "this is me, this is not me"—and other types of self-defining judgments. Should these self-defining judgements suddenly cease, it seems as though the self vanishes with them.

But when the giving up of seeking actually occurs, the self does not die. It just ceases to take center stage as the protagonist or hero of the drama of living. It continues to function as a mediator between the individual and others, but no longer distorts and prevents the integration of experience. When seeking ends, others and the world are experienced through empathic or intuitive embodiment—putting one's self in the place of the other. Should reintegration occur, the divisive, tyrannical conscience is dissolved in love, and is reincorporated along with all other disparate parts of the former self, including the shadow-identity. At this point the psyche as a whole takes care of itself as it unites the inner and outer, the heights and depths, and all of the polarizations that kept it from being one.

The Burden of Expectations

Martha was a young patient in her mid-twenties who could hardly speak due to her extreme introversion and apparent chronic stress reaction. She had drifted from the East to the West Coast, driving her mother's car, and was homeless and without resources. She was unable to give any significant history of trauma, but behaved like someone who had recently escaped from an emotionally abusive situation.

As I discovered over time, for Martha, life was one long abusive experience because she could not meet the social and performance expectations of others. Martha's weakness was a severe lack of social skills and a deep resentment and rebellion against the expectations of others. She preferred to sit on the floor, hiding behind furniture in my office, responding with silence or with great difficulty to my occasional questions.

Martha seemed to me a casualty of our culture. I helped her get on disability because I believed that by removing some cultural expectations for a time she might be more free to explore her own desires and abilities, and possibly find a way to function. Without this freedom she was psychologically paralyzed and probably would become a chronic hospital patient, if she survived at all.

For Martha, seeking to become normal was a dead end. My hope was that a partial release from the tension of seeking and immediate performance demands might allow her to discover a place in society. As I understood her, Martha's only chance of becoming herself, whatever that might be, was to give up trying to become what she thought others wanted her to be. Had she at some point in life developed a strong seeking self, I might have encouraged her to try and give up seeking. But she had been defeated too early, and still needed to develop a seeking self before it could be removed. For someone as weak as her, surrender was impossible; the structure of the mediating self needed to be in place before it could be given up. The last I heard from her, she was living in an isolated cabin in the woods writing poetry.

At best, from the point of view I am suggesting, the seeker is going through a stage of learning, the specific lesson being that he or she cannot by sheer effort and willpower achieve self-transformation. Our culturally-conditioned identity cannot overcome itself by its own efforts, or pull itself up by its own bootstraps. It can only learn this lesson through trying and failing, at which point something more fundamental may emerge. But many individuals, lacking guidance about this alternative of a voluntary or involuntary giving up of seeking, do not seem able to realize this possibility. Instead of giving up the pursuit, they continue on an endless and chronically frustrating quest, become self-destructive, or settle into the recognition of failure with hopeless depression and disillusionment.

An elderly woman came to see me in therapy who was dying of cancer and had chosen not to receive treatment. Her primary concern was dread of the final judgment, imagining herself confronted with the somewhat loose and immoral lifestyle of her youth. I assured this woman that the key to freeing herself from entrapment in this dilemma was accepting herself in the present, and that she would be forgiven only if she could do this. She struggled with this until her death, but was unable to completely forgive herself.

This is not uncommon, and a tragic way to live. This woman was seeking forgiveness, but could not recognize that she alone could unlock the door of her own prison. Her tragedy, like that of so many others, was that her childhood training had led to an inability to accept and love the natural imperfections of her humanity. But she was never able to unambiguously enjoy life—hence, the ongoing concern over her "immoral" lifestyle decades earlier—or accept her inevitable death.

* * *

I am not saying that all seeking is bad, that all seekers inevitably become self-destructive, or that all seeking is futile. In fact, I believe it is necessary for many, and for some it works. But for those

Hate to admit it, don't you?

for whom it does not work and becomes self-defeating, I am suggesting an alternative.

One of the keys to unlocking this dilemma is to be able to objectively evaluate seeking, not as an end in itself, but as a process which may be helpful or not, and which is only useful to a certain point, after which it should be given up. Rather than accepting failure, seekers should be able to consciously and rationally choose another lifestyle, rather than one in which they find themselves imprisoned without the possibility of parole. The only alternative to an impossible search for perfection is learning to live with imperfection.

There is an inherent contradiction in my thinking about this because I believe that it is precisely the strife of the pursuit that allows for the possibility of a relaxation of seeking. One must become divided before one can become whole. A premature giving up of the pursuit may foreclose the intensity and length of strife required to bring about a true giving up, an integration that is all the more powerful because it is involuntary. But the majority of seekers never reach this point. Logically, the prescription of seeking for these individuals might even need to be increased, as they have not suffered enough and have not reached the end of their rope.

The excessive and inappropriate seeking so characteristic of Western culture may be due to a lack of initiation rites, such as American Indians practiced, which required a ritual journey or vision quest away from the tribe. These rites provided the individual with a clear-cut transition and arrival into adulthood. For those who wished to go further, other rites were available, backed by religious experts and the community. These rites were also common in the pre-modern cultures of our ancestors, and for a time may have been effective in some traditional religions. But they no longer seem to work, and modern seekers often feel that they have to make them up haphazardly—or choose to participate in yet another cult of self-realization—in order to find something that does work. This is a forlorn hope, bound to disappoint, because magic no longer works in the modern world. There are no quick fixes, sudden enlightenments, instant transformations, and apparently no divine interventions to save individuals from themselves.

There are some rites of transition in Western culture, such as the transition from school to work, marriage, having children, and some Christian rites and sacraments. But for many these do not seem to be effective in satisfying an individual's needs for an acknowledged place in the community, a healing reunification of the psyche, and the other needs that motivate seeking. This lack of effective initiation rites may be one reason why Western culture is so preoccupied with development and maturity, and one of the most important reasons seekers get into trouble. Without a historical tradition of effective initiation or transition rites, and a profound lack of contemporary guidance, seekers are stumbling through a minefield of potential errors without hope of rescue.

The Dilemma of Transformative Experience

While it is not impossible to experience transformation, it remains impossible to predict its occurrence as a result of any particular conscious effort. Even spiritual disciplines that take a lifetime have an unknown and probably poor record of success. Sometimes they may work precisely because they act as distractions from seeking. For example, certain kinds of meditation and chanting, advocated as spiritual practices, are more hypnotic and meaningless than goal-oriented. This leads me to believe that the road to transformative experience is necessarily unique for each individual, does not require any particular discipline, and cannot be guaranteed or predicted by anything one does to achieve it.

It is not possible to predict the outcome of seeking because negative processes sometimes lead to positive outcomes, and positive processes sometimes lead to negative outcomes. The goals—of which integration is the only realistic one—remain unclear until they are achieved, and often turn out to be quite different than originally imagined. Nevertheless, achieving these goals will be understood—usually in hindsight, and incorrectly—and described to others as resulting from the belief-system and discipline within which they were originally imagined and sought.

No one knows precisely how to achieve transformation, why these experiences occur at a particular time and in a particular manner, or how to adequately describe and understand them, including those who attain them. Those who have experienced these states tend to explain them in the self-serving language of their particular journey. They attempt to universalize their experience in the mistaken belief that others can follow the same path. If there were a valid method, it would soon become universal, and could be studied scientifically. But no such method has yet appeared, though many claim this status.

Language is inadequate to describe transformative experiences, no matter how detailed and sophisticated. There are as many different descriptions of transformation as there are individuals who claim to have experienced it. What has not been experienced cannot be understood through reading about it, so there is little to be gained by reading stories of spiritual journeys, except to realize that certain people have had unusual experiences that they express in their own limited, culturally-determined way. Those who experience transformation while practicing a religious discipline will use the terminology of the discipline to describe and understand their experience, and will tend to minimize personal elements in their description of it. Those who credit success to their own personal and unique efforts sometimes create cults, and prescribe their own style of self-interested striving to their followers.

Several years before my first integrative experience, I was working in a steel mill, and over a period of several weeks was recruited into a Buddhist sect by another worker. As was usual for me, no sooner had I joined, than I dropped out, and did not follow up on the recommended chanting practice, which was supposed to produce not only enlightenment but monetary wealth. Had I continued chanting and then had that same transformative experience, I no doubt would have understood it as a product of Buddhist chanting, and as comprehensible only within the belief-system of the religious discipline I was practicing at the time.

Summary

The points made in this chapter are:

1. Giving up seeking, either through choice or exhaustion, is difficult but recommended as the only antidote to unproductive seeking.

2. The self depends on striving, and fears giving it up as if its life depended on it.

3. An involuntary, transformative giving up of striving ✱ *(below)* requires a kind of burn-out or exhaustion of effort, but without guidance this is a dangerous path to pursue.

4. There is no universal, reliable method of achieving transformation, and no universal, agreed-upon description of the result of transformation, which is a unique process and result for each individual. Rather than a mystical interpretation of "transcendence," transformative experiences may be understood as the natural recovery of unity of the psyche following the exhaustion and removal of culturally-conditioned divisive and self-destructive tendencies.

✱ that's what happened to him so ... is interpreting it "within the belief system of the - discipline he was practicing" den terms." (✓

Wisdom Sample 4

ACCORDING TO the Greek philosopher Epicurus (*c.* 341–270 B.C.E.), disturbances of the soul were caused by *false beliefs* and the *empty desires* or *empty-striving* supported by these false beliefs. Problematic, empty desires were those that were excessive, "puffed up," and that disturbed healthy functioning through preoccupation with longing and useless, draining pursuits. In Martha Nussbaum's description,

> Epicurus sees people rushing about after all sorts of objects of desire: wealth, luxury, power, love, above all immortal life. He is convinced that the central cause of human misery is the disturbance produced by the seemingly "boundless" demands of desire, which will not let us have any rest or stable satisfaction.[1]

Epicurus' solution was the removal of false beliefs that motivated empty desires, and hence the removal of empty desires and the disturbances they caused.

Reacting against what he saw as a corrupt culture, Epicurus modeled healthy human functioning on a hypothetical individual who had not been molded and conditioned by culture and who had the capacity for the good life unaffected by cultural expectations, for example a child or healthy animal. This uncorrupted individual lacked nothing and had no need to seek illusory, culturally-approved goals.

Human desires were of two types, the *natural* and the *empty*. Natural desires were those that occurred in the uncorrupted individual, and empty desires were the artificial products of culture. The "emptiness" of desires was due to their deceitfulness, because they promoted vanity and encouraged endless seeking after unreachable goals, and because they inevitably resulted in self-defeat.

Lucretius (95–52 B.C.E.), a Roman and Epicurean, clearly summarized the problem of empty-striving:

> If only human beings, just as they seem to feel a weight in their minds that wears them out with its heaviness, could also grasp the causes of this and know from what origin such a great mountain of ill stands on their chest, they would hardly lead their lives as we now often see them do, ignorant of what they really want, and always seeking a change of place as if they could put down their burden . . . Thus each person flees himself. But in spite of all his efforts he clings to that self, which we know he never can succeed in escaping, and hates it—all because he is sick and does not know the cause of his sickness.[2]

Like the Epicureans, the Stoics believed that the starting point of philosophy was to become aware of weakness and incapacity concerning the acquisition of the most important things. Whenever an unrealistic ideal was relentlessly pursued, attachment to the ideal led to emotional excess and to the seeker becoming a hostage of the quest. All human beings sought the happy life, but many confused the means to this end, seeking wealth, power, or spirituality for life itself. This led them farther away from life, since the more they indulged in seeking, the farther they got away from what they really desired.

The third school in this tradition, Skepticism, went even further by denying the validity of any choice between good and evil. All beliefs, and valuation in general, were an illness whose symptom was the intense, committed pursuit of a goal. Instead of taking sides and choosing goals to pursue through empty striving, the Skeptic advocated an attitude of inquiry and suspension of judgment. This freed the mind from attachment and commitment to beliefs about what should be sought and what should be avoided. The alternative to seeking, *ataraxia* or peace of mind, could only be obtained through the discipline of the suspension of judgment—refusing the temptation to choose and commit oneself to a one-sided pursuit.

Chapter 4

Positive Disintegration

BELIEFS ABOUT the death and rebirth of the soul figure prominently in esoteric, mystical, and alchemical theories, and similar beliefs have a long history in Christianity and other religions. A psychological version of this theory was set forth by the Polish psychologist, Kazimierz Dabrowski, in his 1964 book, *Positive Disintegration*. Dabrowski described a process in which seeking resulted in the disruption and discarding of the existing personality structure. He found that seeking caused disintegration of the existing structure of the self. The individual was then motivated toward the development of a new self by the lack of a functioning psychic structure, and by attraction toward a new ideal.

In simpler terms, for a new self to emerge, the old self had to die. The way it died was through the process of seeking to improve itself. According to Dabrowski, "In the normal subject disintegration occurs chiefly through the dynamism of the instinct of self-improvement."[1] Dabrowski recognized that disintegration was a byproduct of seeking and was a necessary prelude to reintegration:

The disintegration process, through loosening and even fragmenting the internal psychic environment, through conflicts within the internal environment and with the external environment, is the ground for the birth and development of a higher psychic structure. Disintegration is the basis for developmental thrusts upward, the creation of new evolutionary dynamics, and the movement of the personality to a higher level.[2]

This theory is unusual in its emphasis on the destructive, negative side of seeking; it honestly recognizes that change requires painful destruction as well as reconstruction. According to this theory, as the personality strives toward its ideal through a loosening and fragmentation of the internal environment, two distinct processes come into play—the confirmation and approval of new aims, and the rejection of those elements of the self that seem incompatible with the ideal. Although not recognized in Dabrowski's theory, this process naturally results in the splitting of the psyche into the three elements described in chapter 2—the seeking self, the conscience, and the opposing elements I refer to as the shadow-identity.

The splitting of the psyche results in a state of psychic disorganization and disintegration similar to common mental disorders. But disintegration, according to Dabrowski, is only negative if it fails to contribute to further development—it is otherwise positive and ultimately contributes to mental health. Unfortunately, these disintegrative processes—the dying of the old self through its seeking of a new self—are often misdiagnosed as common mental disorders, because they are not understood as a "positive" process of disintegration. For Dabrowski, these disorders are the way development occurs:

The symptoms of anxiety, nervousness, and psychoneurosis, as well as many cases of psychosis, are often an expression of the developmental continuity. They are processes of positive disintegration . . . slighter forms of mental disorder are closely related to an individual's accelerated development, are often indispensable to it, and, indeed, constitute its essential mechanism.[3]

As Dabrowski elaborates,

The period of real, essential moral maturation is often one of spiritual void: of isolation, loneliness, and misunderstanding. It is the time of the "soul's night," during which the then existing sense of life and forms of connection with life lose their value and force of attraction. The period will close, however, with the working out of an ideal, the arising of a new disposing and directing center, and the appearance of forces of disapproval, shutting out every possibility of a return to the initial level.[4]

Responding to Disintegration

While I agree with this theory and find its emphasis on disintegration refreshing, it underemphasizes the dangers of disintegration. These dangers stem from a widespread misunderstanding of the process and a failure to respond to it appropriately. If the positive potentials of these processes are overlooked or misunderstood, misguided attempts to renew seeking, or self-destructive reactions by the seeker due to severe internal conflict, are likely to result. In the absence of appropriate guidance, which is difficult to find, positive disintegration, though necessary, is a risky business. For example, some who find themselves in disintegrative processes that would have ended in integration, are involuntarily hospitalized and/or medicated, and put under strong social and therapeutic pressure to reverse the disintegrative processes that have them in their grip.

When disintegrative states are treated using standard therapeutic models, the potential for a positive outcome may not be appreciated, and a return to normality may be attempted instead. In this way, a premature renewal of striving after an ideal may be encouraged before the disintegration process is completed. An example of a contemporary therapeutic model that does not recognize the positive potential of disintegration is Heinz Kohut's Self psychology theory. For Kohut, "disintegration anxiety"—a weakness of self due to loss of positive recognition of performance in seeking the ideal—is treated by attempts to strengthen the seeking self.[5] This is done by intellectual distraction from the perceived threat, and a premature attempt to renew the process of striving after an ideal. According to Friedman, "The theme of this treatment is unqualified appreciation of the value and necessity of the patient's strivings."[6] Moreover,

> the patient is induced to continue his project in the face of adversity, and that, according to the theory, is precisely how autonomous structures of self-esteem are built.[7]

According to Kohut, the American self is organized around a quest for ideals in which its performance as heroic seeker is continually monitored by internalized authority figures (Kohut's equivalent of a conscience). This ghostly audience either approves of the performance—thus strengthening the self—or disapproves and withdraws, thus causing "disintegration" or abandonment

anxiety, depression, and other symptoms. Since successful performance is literally required for the survival and cohesion of the self,
there is no alternative but to continue to perform endlessly. Kohut,
like the American culture he mirrors, does not conceive of an end
to seeking, only its eternal renewal.

Dabrowski's theory of positive disintegration also does not
recognize the important possibility that, in some cases, the ideal
has served its purpose and need not be replaced. Since Dabrowski's
goal includes a renewal of seeking—that is, a process of self-
realization, not of transcendence or transformation—he does not
recognize that complete reintegration may occur, in which case
there should be no more need of seeking. Many modern forms of
therapy pursue a similar strategy of strengthening the self by
encouraging a renewal of seeking, rather than reintegration, which
implies and even requires an end of the seeking that preceded it.

Dabrowski's theory is a fairly accurate portrayal of how self-
realization processes repeatedly renew seeking the ideal. Ethical
judgment and moral striving create the conditions necessary for
the creation of a heroic self in quest of the ideal, as well as the
conditions necessary for the consequent onset of disintegration—
a splitting of the self, and avoidance of whatever is incompatible
with the ideal. But it is characteristic of those seeking self-realization that this process is continually renewed.

If accomplished, self-realization does not end disintegration,
but only temporarily strengthens the seeking self and allows it to
renew its vision of an ideal goal. This is the process Dabrowski is
describing. It results in an apparent, but short-lived, reunification—a restoration of the esteem of the seeking self, rather than
unification of the psyche as a whole. A transitional perfection is

recognized that temporarily conceals the imperfection which is always at the core of a human being, and the weakness due to disintegration that is always at the core of the seeking self.

In contrast, the integration that may emerge after striving is given up may be described as "transformative" if it no longer needs the self and its striving, and therefore no longer renews goal-seeking. When a point is reached at which seeking is given up, a complete reintegration may take place based on an absence of the internal splitting and conflicts caused by the seeking self. This is often referred to as the death or transcendence of the seeking self and of its divisiveness. It may also be referred to as salvation, rebirth, grace, enlightenment, or "cosmic consciousness."

What Dabrowski does not recognize is that seeking also supports and maintains the original self, and is used for the purpose of forestalling disintegration. The standard prescriptions for the renewal of seeking are based on the valid assumption that a renewal of seeking results in a strengthening of the original self; this temporarily saves it from disintegration, through revitalized heroics, regardless of whether these efforts are ultimately successful. But strengthening the self in this way is like an addiction, providing temporary benefits that need to be continually renewed with diminishing returns, and, in the long run, catastrophic consequences. Modern psychotherapy generally follows this approach, prematurely resurrecting the quest before it can exhaust itself and end naturally in an involuntary and complete reintegration.

Seeking both constructs and deconstructs the self. If it is believed that seeking will eventually be successful, the self is temporarily affirmed and strengthened. But if it is unsuccessful, the self even more urgently needs the renewal of seeking and the replacement of its ideal. But disintegration may also strengthen the self, by hardening it to suffering and conflict; this eventually results in a kind of stasis or obstinacy that becomes a form of depression, resistant to the recognition of futility and defeat. The process of seeking is, therefore, paradoxical—both constructive and destructive, with the potential to move in either direction. Yet, regardless of the direction of the process, internal conflict continues, and is always the fundamental element that determines how the psyche of the seeker functions and malfunctions.

When disintegration becomes the dominant symptom of seeking, the question then arises as to whether it is preliminary to chronic mental illness or reintegration. The outcome may depend on the availability and expertise of those who help individuals through this relatively unmapped territory. Traditional psychotherapy, for example, may unknowingly encourage chronic mental illness, rather than transformation, by helping to renew seeking prematurely in those on the threshold of an involuntary reintegration.

Seeking is the means by which disintegration occurs and is therefore necessary for transformative states. One is striving to create something, to achieve something. But paradoxically, if successful, the most important accomplishment is destruction of the seeking self and its striving, which obscures and distorts the natural, undivided experience of being fully alive and present to the world.

Following a complete reintegration, the transformed psyche is content with itself for the moment and not divided against itself. It is not prone to seeking because it has no inherent motivation toward change. Transformation is the cure for the beliefs and suffering that underlie and motivate the striving to change. This new integration is, however, likely to fall prey eventually to the renewal of seeking and internal conflict, until it learns to stop re-enacting its culturally-conditioned bad habits.

To prevent this relapse into a renewed cycle of suffering, a new type of self will have to be formed, or discovered—one that recognizes the problem and does not renew seeking or create new heroic selves dependent upon striving. As a first step, the seeker who has been transformed into a nonseeker will have to learn how to avoid seeking, or learn how to seek without dividing the personality into conflicting parts. This may not come easily, and may itself require a type of discipline or deep-seated faith and trust, at least in the beginning.

Summary

The points made in this chapter are as follows:

1. The idea of the death and rebirth of the self has a long history. Various forms of this theory still exist, including the psychological theory of "positive disintegration."

2. Disintegration is a necessary prelude to transformation, and is caused by seeking self-realization or transcendence.

3. Mental illness may indicate a potential transformative process, but is often not recognized as such. Instead, it is inappropriately treated by medication and/or a forced return to normality by a premature renewal of seeking.

4. Once transformation occurs, seeking becomes irrelevant. But seeking may be resurrected because of cultural conditioning and ignorance of transformed states of mind.

Wisdom Sample 5

C H'AN BUDDHISM was the precursor in China of Zen Buddhism which later flourished in Japan. The founder of Ch'an
Buddhism was Bodhidharma, an Indian teacher. Around 500 C.E.,
Bodhidharma journeyed to China and visited the Emperor Wu, a
devout Buddhist, who boasted to Bodhidharma of his accomplish-
ments:

> "I have built many temples. I have copied the sacred sutras. I have
> led many to the Buddha. Therefore, I ask you: What is my merit:
> What reward have I earned?" Bodhidharma reportedly growled,
> "None whatsoever, your Majesty." The emperor was startled but
> persisted, "Tell me then, what is the most important principle or
> teaching of Buddhism?" "Vast emptiness," Bodhidharma replied,
> meaning, of course, the void of nonattachment. Not knowing
> what to make of his guest, the emperor backed away and inquired,
> "Who exactly are you who stands before me now?" To which
> Bodhidharma admitted he had no idea.[8]

Ch'an Buddhism died out in China around 1300 C.E. What is
known about it exists mainly in the form of brief stories about
spiritual masters whose actions sought to destroy the intellectual
processes which kept their disciples from attaining enlightenment.
These disciples commonly achieved enlightenment by exhausting
themselves on an unsolvable problem or *koan* given to them by a
master, or by having a master suddenly reframe their experience
so they realized the futility of seeking.

As long as there was a conscious intention of attaining something, an obstacle was in the way. Thoughts must flow spontaneously rather than through the coercion of concentration on a goal, or on the moral evaluation of good and evil. When both the means of expression and the roots of mental activity were destroyed, only then was enlightenment possible. True reality was discovered in the imperfection and incompletion of the individual.

Such a narrative of a sudden enlightenment appears in *The Gateless Pass* (*c*. 1200 C.E.):

Nan-ch'uan was asked by Chao-Chu, "What is the Way?" Ch'uan replied, "The everyday mind is the Way." Chou then asked, "Can one still be inclined to pursue it or not?" Ch'uan replied, "To intentionally pursue it is in fact to go against it." Chou then asked, "If there is no intention, then how do you know it is the Way?" To which Ch'uan replied, "The Way does not belong to the things that are known, nor does it belong to the things that are unknown. If you 'know' it, you are incorrectly enlightened; but of what you do not know, no notice is made. If you genuinely fathom the unquestionable Way, it is like the sky unrestrictedly opening up wide and clear. How do you force this to be 'right' or 'wrong'?" When these words were finished, Chou was suddenly enlightened.[9]

Zen Buddhism asserts that there is no purpose in life, and the virtue of any process is in its unhurriedness and naturalness. The forced striving of Westerners and those who seek enlightenment is one of the problems addressed by the paradoxical discourse of Zen. Forced striving results "when the process is emphasized, the end is forgotten, and process itself comes to be identified with the end."[10]

The gesture of letting go cannot be made with ulterior motives, because then it will not take into account the actual, inner condition. The person who has accomplished the task of devalorization of every ideal no longer pursues values in a compulsive manner.

Chapter 5

The Never Ending Quest

The Progressive Developmental Paradigm
and the Pursuit of the Normative Ideal

IN ADDITION to exploring the psychology of the seeking self, this book offers a critical examination of a fundamental value of American culture, which I have named the *progressive developmental paradigm*. This is the belief system underlying most types of seeking. It assumes that development is always positive, and that efforts toward self-improvement will always be productive and worthwhile.

I undertake this critique because of the harm this belief system causes to individuals, society, and the natural environment.[1] One specific focus of this critique is on the use of this paradigm in the psychological literature, especially the self-help and psychotherapy literatures, and how the paradigm promotes a normative *self-construct* that is divided against itself and others in a futile and self-destructive pursuit of illusions.

Appending the term *construct* to the term *self*, as above, refers to a belief-system about the self. This is not to say that there is a literal self apart from beliefs about it, but this distinction is helpful in reminding the reader that the selves I specifically refer to are essentially belief-systems.

As we have seen, seeking is both a symptom and cause of mental illness. But the recognition of this problem and how to treat

modernism

it—a problem pervasive in modern culture for at least the last three hundred years, and in less extreme forms in both Western and Eastern cultures for at least the last three thousand years—is sadly deficient.[2] A different attitude toward those disintegrative states that are potentially transformative would reduce suffering, and allow more positive treatment outcomes, for those on the verge of transformation. Yet most current treatments only offer reactive, premature attempts—for example, "brief therapies"—to find a cure for internal conflict and disintegration through renewed striving.

The understanding necessary for developing a critical attitude toward seeking is extremely rare in American culture. The endless parade of success stories told about Americans via every type of media results in a thorough indoctrination from birth to death in the value of the progressive developmental paradigm. But I would rather convince the reader that the progressive developmental paradigm is an archetypal "false belief" that encourages "empty desires," "empty striving," and the phenomenon of an "empty self."[3]

The modern concept of development has many definitions according to its use and abuse in various fields of thought. The definition of development that I examine here, using the term "progressive developmental paradigm," is one that emphasizes positive psychological or spiritual change with an aspirational component, through which the concept of development provides meaning and purpose to the individual. This is the fundamental belief of the seeking self that underlies all specific attempts at seeking.

Aspirational evaluations associated with the progressive developmental paradigm promote the desire to grow and to reach appropriate milestones on the path toward gaining the control, freedom, and recognition associated with an ideal, adult self-construct, or whatever other ideal may be sought. Development functions as an explanatory and guiding framework for pursuit of an improved or ideal self-construct. It sanctions the actions of the pursuing self, which becomes heroic and valued through its self-serving and self-sacrificial quest.

Aspirational evaluations have their historical roots in the pursuit of spirituality and salvation, and these inherent associations strengthen the eloquence of the paradigm in its various modern secular applications. These progressive evaluations, with transcendent and perfectionistic overtones in their language and suggested outcomes, are especially common in the self-help literature.

The progressive developmental paradigm is oriented toward ideals in general, but especially the *normative-ideal*, which is the model the culture provides its members so that they can cope and survive in society. As the survival of the self is usually believed to require this pursuit, the goal of the normative-ideal is not questioned by the majority, but rather supported by whatever means, arguments, and techniques that are necessary. Even those who attempt to be different and unique individuals are oriented by and reacting to the normative-ideal, thereby becoming a variation of its theme.

The normative-ideal, however, is far from "normal" or average, but is informed by successive heroic and celebrity models that give it new twists and turns, and determine its current cosmetic features. The normative-ideal is often perfectionistic, as exemplified by the very slim and youthful female models who have inspired so many diets and eating disorders among women, and by the male muscle-builder who kicks sand in the face of his skinny rival on the beach.

The normative-ideal has a twofold function. First, it justifies the process of self-domination in pursuit of an ideal. Second, it justifies and encourages the compliance of individuals with the ideal values that the wider culture seeks to maintain and replicate. For example, as Nikolas Rose notes in *Governing the Soul*,

> Through self-inspection, self-problematization, self-monitoring, and confession, we evaluate ourselves according to the criteria provided for us by others. Through self-reformation, therapy, techniques of body alteration, and the calculated reshaping of speech and emotion, we adjust ourselves by means of the techniques propounded by the experts of the soul. The government of the soul depends upon our recognition of ourselves as ideally and potentially certain sorts of person, the unease generated by a normative judgment of what we are and could become, and the incitement offered to overcome this discrepancy by following the advice of experts in the management of the self.[4]

The normative-ideal is whatever the current culture defines as an appropriate, acceptable, or ideal self-construct. Given the modern tendency to compartmentalize, the same individual may have several normative-ideals, for example, separate performance ideals for religiosity, social life, family, work, and recreation.

The seeking self-construct is a retrospective reconstruction that vindicates itself through pursuit of the normative-ideal. The pursuit of ideals is basic to personal identity and provides a historical story of striving that gives coherence and continuity to the self-construct. This history tells the tale of the successes and failures of the self-interested pursuits of the self-construct, which merit confirmation or rejection by the taskmaster conscience and by others.

The pursuit of an object or goal, no matter how often the goal is achieved, is recreated in successive pursuits by a self that is motivated, at least in part, by cultural ideals. Advertising, for example, implies a lack of perceived happiness, perfection, or fulfillment, the absence of which is necessary to motivate the quest for ideal goals. Seeking attempts to conceal the perceived lack of fulfillment through preoccupation with ideals that promise future fulfillment by means of individual effort and moral compliance.

To the extent that the history of the self-construct can be positively framed, particularly as a masterful agent overcoming obstacles on the path to its ultimate success, the self is maintained. The culturally-conditioned absence, or sense of imperfection which drives the quest, can be safely ignored so long as the progressive interpretation of the autobiography of the seeking self-construct remains intact.

Falling into the Sky

Over time, the pursuit of the normative-ideal becomes a flight from recognition and awareness of the seeker's lack of integration. In essence, seeking turns its face away from the splitting and internal conflict that is created by the pursuit itself. Striving also fails to recognize the futility of a pursuit in which the good is always just out of reach or around the corner, so that one is neither here nor there. As long as the seeker is fleeing from a rejected self in pursuit of an ideal self-construct, the seeker is an emptiness craving fulfillment, a ghost in limbo between illusions.

One of the most common reasons ghosts are believed to return to haunt places and individuals is that they have unfinished business—they cannot leave the earth until they complete their quest. This idea also applies to those who get caught up in an unending quest while still alive. As a result of seeking, they begin to lose their substance and become detached from the earth; but at the same time, they frantically try to return to it and finish living their lives. *pretas*

Yet it is precisely their quest that prevents them from regaining their ground. As the poet Hölderlin wrote, "It is possible to fall into the heights, as well as into the depths." As seekers "fall into the sky"—that is, become ungrounded due to their upward-oriented seeking—they panic, grasping for a hold on life, but only ascend more quickly as a result of their frantic efforts. Even redirecting their striving toward becoming grounded or "real" inevitably becomes a quest that maintains their lack of groundedness in life.

This is an important reason why the seeking self sometimes appears to be caught up in an out-of-body experience: it seems both a lost soul seeking reincarnation, and an empty body looking for a shaman to return its lost soul. More often than not, the disembodied self observes only the surface of the body, concerned about its appearance and performance, as if it lived in the mirror rather than in the body itself. From above the body, the conscience and reason dominate the emotions and sensations—the head over heart and desire—creating the vertical mind/body split of the modern American self. In this mind/body split, it is notable that the soul, having been lost for at least several centuries, is no longer even part of the equation.

By its efforts, the ungrounded, seeking self is always in a process of becoming more and more ghost-like and disconnected—lost and dissociated from the body and the natural unity of experience. The goal it seeks hovers above, just out of reach in the heavens, where illusory perfection dwells. The seeking self progressively approximates the ghost-like, ideal self-construct by itself becoming illusory and ghostlike. Then, in belated reaction to recognition of its emptiness, the disembodied self attempts to ground itself through defensive operations driven by anxiety, depression, and avoidance of self-awareness.

* * *

Peter, formerly a successful, married father, was accused of resisting arrest and assaulting police officers, who had responded to a false complaint of domestic violence. As a result, Peter lost his job and was separated from his wife and daughter. He drank heavily and used drugs while living on the street, waiting for the courts to prosecute him.

Seriously depressed and distraught, Peter sought help in therapy. He was seeking desperately to return to the normal life he had before he lost control. His attitude swung from being self-destructive, to being resigned to his fate, to being hopeful for a positive outcome. Each tendency became dominant in turn as he obsessively processed what had happened, what was happening, and what might happen. Peter needed to slow down, relax, face what was to come, and make the best of it in order to be able to cope as effectively as possible.

I tried to help him cope effectively and to reduce his suffering. However, I realized that he was causing this suffering himself by seeking to repair a situation that was out of his control. Together we formulated a psychological explanation for his behavior before and during the incident for which he was charged. Over time, Peter came to understand that he had been, and still was, trying too hard in seeking his ideals, and that he tended to overreact to obstacles. He could now see this tendency at work during the incident for which he was charged, and became determined to restrain himself from such overreactions in the future.

Summary

The points made in this chapter are the following:

1. The progressive developmental paradigm, or belief in progressive development, is the belief system of the seeker.

2. The normative-ideal is the standard cultural model for the ideal self-construct. Seeking the normative-ideal sustains the culture and the self within the culture.

3. Seeking is potentially a disease if its disintegrating effects become chronic and do not result in transformation. But seeking is also constructive, as it supports the self by providing it with a reason for being, and a way of affirming its apparent value—as a heroic seeker—despite its lacks and faults.

4. The self survives disintegration by continually renewing its progressive developmental agendas of seeking, but this is only a stopgap, a false reunification, and not a solution to the problems that led to, and are associated with, seeking. Survival guarantees a continuation of the problem, not its solution.

5. Seeking produces a horizontal split in the psyche, between above and below, resulting in an ungrounded, ghost-like self whose efforts to become real only cause it to more rapidly become lost and "fall into the sky."

Historical Example 1: John Bunyan

J OHN BUNYAN (1628–1688) wrote the most influential Protestant manual of his time, *The Pilgrim's Progress*, and was an expert, based on his own experience, on the religious problem of obsession. *Obsession* was distinguished from *possession*—identification with a demon or Satan—in that the obsessed victim was harassed by an external demon. In Bunyan's case, he was harassed by the voice of Satan.

Bunyan later wrote a book on how Satan attacked every Christian. Satan—in psychological terms, his shadow-identity and taskmaster conscience—attacked Bunyan by putting doubt in his mind about the truthfulness of the scriptures and about whether he was saved or "elected." Bunyan's primary defense against these attacks, which came in waves over several years, was the Bible, but some parts of the Bible only increased his doubts. He relates his internal conflict:

> Neither as yet could I attain to any comfortable persuasion that I had faith in Christ, but instead of having satisfaction here I began to find my soul to be assaulted with fresh doubts about my future happiness; especially with such as these, "whether I was elected; but how if the day of grace should be past and gone?"
>
> By these two temptations I was very much afflicted and disquieted; sometimes by one and sometimes by the other of them. And first, to speak of that about my questioning my election, I found at this time, that though I was in a flame to find the way to heaven and glory, and thought nothing could beat me

off from this, yet this question did so offend and discourage me, that I was, especially sometimes, as if the very strength of my body also had been taken away by the force and power thereof. This Scripture did also seem to me to trample upon all my desires: "it is neither in him that willeth, nor in him that runneth; but in God that showeth mercy."

With this Scripture I could not tell what to do; for I evidently saw, unless that the great God, of his infinite grace and bounty, had voluntarily chosen me to be a vessel of mercy, though I should desire, and long, and labor until my heart did break, no good could come of it. . . . Why, then, said Satan, you had as good leave off, and strive no farther; for if indeed, you should not be elected and chosen of God, there is no hope for your being saved.[5]

To *not* seek seemed a temptation of Satan, and Bunyan believed it better to be a martyr to his cause through continued seeking than to admit failure or impotence. For Bunyan, aflame with the enthusiasm of the seeker, the discipline of faith was too passive. Passive faith did not mirror the standard themes of the religious quest in which a heroic self overcame all obstacles to salvation, and—by the merit of its efforts—was granted deserved grace and saved.

It is likely that Bunyan's distress and confusion about these matters was common. Despite the authority of the Bible and of some religious leaders who defined sin as self-interested or prideful seeking, to question the ability of the will to seek salvation seemed defeatist, a temptation of the devil, rather than an essential clue, reminding Bunyan of what he already knew intellectually—that he was in fact not a god, and could not determine his own fate.

Reflecting on his own spiritual dilemma, Bunyan wrote *The Pilgrim's Progress*, a manifesto for the taskmaster conscience, guiding the striving of the Christian hero on a romantic quest to obtain salvation.

The Christian version of progressive development, seeking salvation, was in many ways as problematic as the modern secular versions of the paradigm, and resulted in many casualties and martyrs to its cause. The sufferings of those seekers later sanctified by the Church provide numerous case histories of the dangers and self-destructiveness associated with spiritual striving. But instead of being understood as warnings, this extreme suffering was overlooked or interpreted as evidence confirming extraordinary self-sacrifice, which justified the naming of a spiritual exemplar.

The Protestant Church began with Martin Luther's (1483–1546) rebellion against Catholicism. One of Luther's most important insights was that seeking salvation was not only useless, but sinful. Grace was a gift of God and could not be won by human effort of any kind. John Calvin (1509–1564) followed Luther closely in denying the ability of the will to successfully seek salvation.

Bunyan was well aware of this tradition of thought about grace, with its roots in the teachings of Saint Paul and Saint Augustine, and had even advocated it in pamphlets against its detractors. Yet he was so thoroughly conditioned to seeking, in his own spiritual crisis, he could only experience this point of view as a shadow-identity—the devil tempting him to give up faith in his own ability to successfully win salvation. For Bunyan, to stop seeking would have meant to die psychologically, an unacceptable proposition. But what Bunyan did not fully understand was that this death was necessary to receive grace—that is, reintegration—

and that to continue seeking, which according to Luther and Calvin was a manifestation of the sin of pride, was to prevent God from freely giving him grace.

Wisdom Sample 6

M ARTIN LUTHER, an Augustinian monk, nailed ninety-five theses for discussion to the door of the church of Wittenburg in Saxony in 1517. Thus began the Reformation that led to Protestantism and nearly all of the other modern non-Catholic forms of Christianity. Luther had a troubled soul and had failed to find peace even though he diligently strove for grace. His experience contradicted those who taught that free will was sufficient to avoid evil, follow divine ethical commands, love God, and obtain grace. Luther's spiritual torment led him to pursue a doctorate in theology and continue to seek ways to cleanse himself of sin. Finally, he came to understand that righteousness cannot be obtained by striving or merit, but is freely given by God to the faithful.

Luther subsequently published *The Bondage of the Will* (1525), in which he denied the value and place of spiritual striving to obtain grace. For Luther, this point of view was central, the heart of the gospel and the foundation of faith. The original, crucial question for the Reformation was whether Christianity was to be a religion of complete reliance on God for salvation or whether it would endorse self-reliance and self-serving effort as a means to win salvation.

Luther attacked the humanistic ideals of rational self-control and self-sufficiency in theology, through which it was considered possible to find and know God by the use of unaided reason. This natural theology, which had come to prominence during the Renaissance and later strongly influenced the Christian Church, promoted the seeking of spirituality. According to Luther, however, it was bankrupt, and would only lead to separation from God. Luther felt compelled to expose this theology as a product of the pride of helpless sinners who denied their own helplessness. It was a debate about means, not ends.

According to Luther, the individual, through both original sin and subsequent sinning, had ceased to be good, had no power to please God (and thus influence his or her fate), and could do nothing but continue in sin. Reason was blind and the will hostile to God. Since all that was done was sinfully motivated, no possibility of merit existed, and the exercise of choice was enslaved to sin. Luther's experience of revelation was recognition of the truth of this argument, that he had been saved *in spite of himself.* As Luther summarized his position,

Man, before he is created to be man, does and endeavors nothing towards his being made a creature, and when he is made and created he does and endeavors nothing towards his continuance as a creature; both his creation and his continuance come to pass by the sole will of the omnipotent power and goodness of God, Who creates and preserves us without ourselves. Yet God does not work in us without us; for He created and preserves us for this very purpose, that He might work in us and we might cooperate with Him, whether that occurs outside His kingdom, by His general omnipotence, or within His kingdom, by the special power of His Spirit. So, too, I say that man, before he is renewed into the new creation of the Spirit's kingdom, does and endeavors nothing to prepare himself for that new creation and kingdom, and when he is re-created he does and endeavors nothing towards his perseverance in that kingdom; but the Spirit alone works both blessings in us, regenerating us, and preserving us when regenerate, without ourselves . . . But He does not work in us without us, for He re-created and preserves us for this very purpose, that He might work in us and we might cooperate with Him. Thus he preaches, shows mercy to the poor, and comforts the afflicted by means of us. But what is hereby attributed to 'free-will'? What, indeed, is left it but—nothing! In truth, nothing![16] *False disjunction*

Free will is both God + Satan

Two hundred years later, John Wesley, the founder of Methodism, completely undermined Luther's doctrine by suggesting that all Christians could become sanctified, thereby freeing their will to pursue salvation. For the sanctified, "whatsoever is done by their hands, the Father, who is in them, He doeth the works." Thus, for Wesley, the sanctified Christian should always be actively seeking to do, and to be, good.[7]

However, as Luther had made clear, it was all too easy to presume sanctification. Just as Catholics had assumed under the guise of sacramental sanctification, Protestants were also severely tempted to assume that they had already received grace, and that, consequently, whatever they did—including the seeking of perfection—was automatically sanctioned by God. This is clearly the assumption that justified Bunyan's fictional quest and model of Christian striving. This same assumption was later codified and dogmatized by Wesley, and subsequently by several other branches of Protestantism.

A century after Wesley, similar progressive developmental belief-systems were secularized and codified in the documents founding the new democracy of the United States. Seeking self-fulfillment, self-realization, and transcendence became the norma-tive-ideal model for all those who believed in the American Dream. Henceforth, to oppose this point of view was un-American.

Chapter 6

The Self and its Strivings

AS A FRESHMAN in junior college I was placed in an advanced English class. On our first day, the assignment was to write an essay during class entitled "Who am I?" The class was taught by two teachers, and I received the two highest grades for the essay—F+ and D- —because I criticized the assignment, saying that there was no way to describe one's self. This is not to say that most people don't try, but they will usually get an F for their efforts. The self-construct is often defined in terms of what the person does, has done, and intends to do, as if these deeds and intentions needed an author and reason for being. This self-construct serves as a convenient fiction that is continuously altered according to need and circumstance.

The self-construct consists of what individuals *represent* themselves to be, and this representation is often distorted in a self-serving and self-confirming way. The form of the self-construct is created by combining selected memories into an autobiographical drama of striving:

> If a major aspect of personality is the story we construct of our lives, then self-defining memories and personal strivings are the raw material of that story. Personal strivings or long-term goals are the outlines we sketch for our life stories to follow.[1]

Inevitable inconsistencies between one's self-image and external feedback, and between one's self-construct and ideal standards, motivate the emergence of self-completion strategies and the desire for change. Personal striving toward long-term goals always reflects the ideals and heroic myths of the culture. Because the self understands itself as a history of striving, it has difficulty imagining itself as not striving, except under rare circumstances of great success.

The dilemma posed by seeking is that the present self, which is rejected in favor of an ideal self-construct, can only redeem itself by striving to become like the ideal. But this becomes a formula for disaster, as the original self usually fails in this effort, and thus is caught in a trap of its own making from which it cannot escape. Within this trap, the only partial relief available is to maintain the *appearance* of progress toward becoming the ideal as long as possible, and in this way to hypocritically avoid exposure as a failure and experience psychological death.

The seeking self disintegrates when it cannot maintain the appearance of successful striving. Consequently, in order to survive, the self will pretend to be successful in its seeking in order to prevent other people—and especially itself—from recognizing its inability to make progress toward the ideal. The symptom of this inability that could eventually lead to transformation—the disintegration of the self—is interrupted by a renewal of striving to regain self-worth. This seems like a reasonable response, but results in an endless renewal of unproductive and self-destructive seeking without resolution.

Self-Domination

This exhausting cyclic struggle of continual self-renewal is promoted by Western culture, and failure or abandonment of the struggle is considered inappropriate or even sick. The psychology of the self seeking the normative-ideal is partly based on a belief that can be summed up, "if I don't dominate myself, someone else will"—for example, parents, police, big brother, employers, competitors, and so on. Moreover, by dominating myself, I identify with and mirror the dominant other, thereby protecting myself in part from the disapproval and aggression of the other. Other partial motivations for the psychology of the seeking self include its quest to be loved and its fear of abandonment.

Belief and engagement in progressive developmental quests, as a response to personal embarrassment and failure, obeys the critical expectations and demands of others, whether only imagined or actually perceived. Seeking thus becomes a way to avoid a feared, complete dominance by others. The helpless and inadequate child first experiences domination by his or her parents. Later, the young adult is dominated by the cultural expectations expressed through educational, religious, vocational, and other institutions. Submission is reinforced by frequent reminders of the fate of those who do not conform: prison, involuntary hospitalization and treatment, or homelessness without shelter, security, or support—the life of a victim awaiting further abuse.

In order to avoid this fate and demonstrate one's success, especially when it is only an imitation of success, the questing individual often must engage in selfish manipulation of significant and subordinate others. This tactic allows the seeker to obtain confirmation of the value of the self through power over others, and to impose upon them a similar quest. Through identification with the aggressor, who demands obedience to expectations or goal-oriented change, dominated individuals will inevitably pass on and repeat the pattern of domination by self-righteously dominating others. Most children, for example, seem to consciously or unconsciously inherit the burden of the failed quests of their parents.

In this psychology, there seem to be three options: 1) to be loved by others, 2) to be dominated by others, or 3) to dominate oneself in order to win the love and avoid the domination of others. A fourth option—complete rejection and abandonment by others, as the traditional scapegoat exorcised from the community— looms as a possibility, and further encourages self-domination.

The modern American self-construct is imagined as creating itself, managing its development, and owning the product—the self thus "owns" itself. The self-construct is "promoted" by demonstrated self-reliance and maturity to the position of self-monitor, self-manager, and self-therapist. However, this promotion does not mean that the self is free. On the contrary, it is even more closely shaped according to expectations and determined by the cultural context. It becomes, in effect, its own enforcer of obedience, and the judge of its failure or success in meeting these expectations. From this structure and dynamic, it is clear that the self-construct is closely identified with its taskmaster conscience, which operates under the cultural guidance of specific developmental agendas.

The progressive developmental paradigm serves the self through two functions. The first function involves restraining, containing, and delaying inappropriate desire through self-sacrifice or sublimation. The second, or defensive function protects the self against negative evaluation by others as being inadequate or unlovable, and therefore subject to domination or rejection. As a defensive strategy, this paradigm acknowledges imperfection at the same time that it promises future perfection. The self becomes worthy because it takes responsibility for its defects. It acknowledges the potential for devaluation by others and their related demands for change, thus allowing for the domination of the self in their stead by the conscience. At the same time, self-esteem and a sense of personal superiority is supported by self-sacrificial striving toward improvement, which promises genuine approval by others.

The self-construct and its progressive developmental biography are the means by which the individual is controlled and harnessed by institutions. Individuals who fail or who otherwise deviate from institutional norms for the seeker often fall into various categories of mental illness, or join an underclass of inferior, scapegoated individuals.

These scapegoated individuals, who have been prevented or disallowed the opportunity of progressive development in various ways, are goaded into misbehaviors that preoccupy the media and populate the prisons, implying that if the individual does not behave or seek appropriately, he or she will also be removed from society. A belief in progressive development eventually leads the seeker to competition for power and prestige, driven by a need for approval from others, that increasingly lacks restraint in both means and ends.

Guarding the Self

Phyllis, a female police officer, came to me for psychological assessments of her two oldest children, Katrina, twelve, and Brad, ten. She recounted the story of her long, abusive relationship with her previous husband. She had been the primary victim, but the children were periodically in danger as well. Phyllis had coped with this threat by becoming a policewoman. Now, married to the chief of police, she patrolled daily the area where they lived, protecting herself and her children from their former abuser, who was separated from the family, but still lived in town. Phyllis was concerned about the mental health of her oldest children, who seemed anxious and preoccupied at times. After hearing her story and talking to her children, it was clear to me that they, in their own ways, followed their mother's example.

While her mother was being abused, Katrina had protected the younger children. They would often go to a tree house where they felt safe from the abuser. Once they actually fended him off when he tried to climb up to their perch. Now every evening before going to sleep, Katrina walks to the front door of their house and scans the neighborhood for signs of this man. She is extremely capable, an "A" student, and participates in many creative activities with great success.

By becoming a "substitute mother" when necessary, and by excelling in school and in other creative activities, Katrina may have felt that she was protecting herself and her family. Her younger brother, Brad, likewise excelled in sports, and protected himself by becoming strong and skilled in competition. Both children were intelligent and well-liked.

On the surface these were admirable kids, but underneath they were overly anxious, overly serious, and unable to be carefree and playful like most of their friends. They were driven, unhappy overachievers. In essence, they were constantly seeking new goals and ways to impress themselves and others with two fundamental messages. First, they were able to take care of and protect themselves; second, they were worthy of protection and love by the adults who admired them. They were examples of how the traumas of life lead to progressive developmental seeking that interferes with normal living. They learned too early the progressive developmental lesson that performance is more important than play.

Katrina and her brother were too busy preparing to protect themselves from further abuse to enjoy their childhood. It is likely that this pattern of coping if untreated could haunt them into adulthood and even lead to major mental illness, such as "nervous breakdowns." Because of their preoccupation with performance, no matter how successful they may be, they will have difficulty in relationships because of an inability to accept weakness or imperfection in themselves and others, and their consequent inability to relax and enjoy life and relationships.

Progressive developmental solutions to traumas in terms of mastery, positive change, and preparedness are not always what they seem to be. They may by their very success burden the individual with a style of coping that later haunts and re-traumatizes the individual. I encouraged Phyllis to recognize her children's problems in herself, and to begin to model a more relaxed and less hypervigilant lifestyle for her children. I also gave her information to read on traumatic reactions and how they shape identity.

The Irony of "Self-Mastery"

Trauma in its various forms has been found to be one of the most common causes of mental illness. One way of understanding responses to trauma is in the contrast between those who are relatively successful in "mastering the trauma" and those who are not. Those who are unsuccessful may be said to develop a "victim-identity," because, for them, the trauma remains unresolvable and continues to recur. Those who respond "successfully" to traumas may be free of recurrences of trauma, but remain burdened with the excessive mental skills developed to cope with the original trauma. These skills may become an unrecognized form of mental illness which masquerade as strengths rather than weaknesses because they are closely associated with the progressive developmental paradigm.

In this way, the admired mastery becomes a captivity to a "successful" form of coping, rather than captivity to an unsuccessful form of coping, as occurs in the victim-identity. The original trauma is replaced by the coping mechanism, including in the case of Phyllis' children, the requirement of perfect performances, success in all endeavors, pleasing adults all of the time, and the need to be frequently reassured that they are loved and will be safe. Because this coping mechanism becomes fixed and unalterable— a requirement for the maintenance of identity—the coping mechanism itself becomes traumatic through compulsive repetition.

For the victim-identity, the traumatic scenario is repeated or re-created because of vulnerability and a need for mastery of the problem. For the precocious identity, the trauma continues. That is because the original coping mechanism, which results in successful mastery, has developed a life of its own. The rigid, conditioned coping mechanism becomes hostile and counterproductive to appropriate change, as well as to its own removal or alteration. The coping mechanism becomes *automatic*. It will not let the person rest or move on to other appropriate styles of coping, and also prevents the kind of recreation and play that is a natural and necessary counterpoint to seeking.

Precocious children are often admired by parents and teachers who become devoted to them, even idolize them, because they are gifted and talented and represent their own unrealized desires. But because of this narcissistic devotion, the child will be fearful of disappointing parents and teachers, and consequently will even more desperately strive for achievement, which becomes a survival mechanism. The ideal identity imposed on them, and subsequently expected if not demanded, does not lead to love of the child, but to love (mixed with envy, regret, and anger) of the imposed ideal. When due to past trauma and hypersensitivity, the threat of abandonment and abuse begin to loom on the horizon, performance in mimicking the imposed ideal necessarily replaces play. There is no time for relaxation, and little time for rest.

These children develop a harsh and unforgiving taskmaster conscience. They are inevitably disillusioned by the inadequacies of their parents, who not only fail to completely protect and nurture them, but also fail to model the ideals they imposed on their children. When disillusioned in this way, they tend to develop even more rigid and unalterable ideal goals that profoundly distort and sometimes stunt subsequent developmental experiences. They reject and avoid all elements in their lives not related to the immediate performance concerns necessary for pleasing the narcissistic needs of others.

Once these coping patterns become habits, there is little room for relaxation and enjoyment because the precocious lifestyle imposed on these children endlessly renews performance demands. If they enjoy reasonable success, they may seem to be relatively well adjusted, but will still be driven within by ghosts from their past—the ideal expectations of parents, teachers, and other authority figures. If not successful, they may suffer from various forms of chronic mental illness, or seek shortcuts, such as cheating, stealing, dealing and/or taking drugs, or resorting to violence. In any case, personal fulfillment will always seem to be beyond their reach because the needs of others must be satisfied first.

These two coping styles in response to trauma—victim identity and precocious identity—are relevant to understanding the difficulties faced by all seekers. While all individuals experience traumas, some fall under the culturally conditioned response of seeking, over which they lose control. They subsequently become the captives of their own internalized coping responses, and assume that others will not love them unless they perform these responses as they always have.

Narcissism and the Search for Self-Acceptance

A specific type of trauma, called *narcissistic trauma*, has been very prevalent in the psychology literature since the 1970s. Translated into the language used here, narcissistic trauma usually results from the frustration of the seeker who fails to become the ideal. Within the last thirty years, these narcissistic tendencies and their associated symptoms and conflicts have been recognized as one of the most common mental illnesses plaguing the modern

American self. An example of this modern mental illness, associated with the progressive developmental paradigm, is evident in the portrayal by Elan Golomb of narcissistic parents. These parents

> unconsciously deny an unstated and intolerably poor self-image through inflation. They turn themselves into glittering figures of immense grandeur surrounded by psychologically impenetrable walls. The goal of this self-deception is to be impervious to greatly feared external criticism and to their own roiling sea of doubts. This figure of paradox needs to be regarded as perfect by all. To achieve this, he or she constructs an elaborate persona . . . [which] needs an appreciative audience to applaud it. If enough people do so, the narcissist is relieved that no one can see through his disguise. The persona is a defensive schema to hide behind . . . Behind the grandiose parading, the narcissist feels empty and devoid of value. Because his life is organized to deny negative feelings about himself and to maintain an illusion of superiority, the narcissist's family is forcibly conscripted into supporting roles.[2]

The child of a narcissist has no choice but to live out the unfulfilled desires of the parent. These desires are projected onto the child and may be idealizing or depreciating, often alternating between the two, but always overwhelming the child's own perspective, needs, and choices in regard to the self-determination of identity.

Whether the projection is that of a defect or an excellence, the child is subject to an endless series of intrusive interventions by the parent demanding improvement and making acceptance and love contingent on fulfilling parental expectations: "The narcissistic press for symbiotic unity requires that the perceptions of the child and parent be identical."[3] As Golomb writes,

> Since the child is the carrier of the narcissistic parents' perceived but rejected imperfections and grandiose fantasies, his self-image is disturbingly contradictory . . . Whatever the parent feels is his or her problem is transplanted into the child . . . and subjected to an endless campaign of reform to obtain some worth.[4]

Children of narcissists learn to feel that a perfect performance that fulfills the needs of the significant other is necessary for acceptance and love. But the outcome of this performance is a feeling that they have no right to exist, since becoming a separate person is a betrayal of the significant other—a reaction they have experienced repeatedly with their narcissistic parents. Neither good nor bad performances result in a sustained acceptance: "Each narcissistic parent in each generation repeats the crime that was perpetrated against him. The crime is nonacceptance."[5] This style of relationship is then taken up by the child:

> The child of a narcissist who emulates his parent is always trying to improve the other person. This is what his parents did to him and to everyone else. As an act of identification with his parents, he responds to people's errors with the kind of rage his parents showered on him. He wants to accept people as they are and has been repeatedly told to do so but feels inner pressure to correct.[6]

The emotional root of narcissism and of the drive toward self-improvement is shame. Shame triggers repression and internal conflict and underlies the pathology of the seeking self. Shame is the opposite of genuine self-love and self-acceptance.

Summary

The points made in this chapter are as follows:

1. The self-construct is based on a story consisting of selected memories of striving, arranged in the sequence of a quest for ideal goals.

2. In order to maintain positive relationships and avoid depression and disintegration, the self will pretend progress in striving and deceive itself and others about problems with striving.

3. In the process of striving, the self dominates itself to assure success, and sometimes dominates others to assure recognition of striving or to conceal failure.

4. When an individual attempts to master a past trauma or seek protection from future traumas, the result may be a fixed pattern of seeking to please others or to perform perfectly, which is itself traumatic.

Historical Example 2: Paul Schreber (1842–1911)

PAUL SCHREBER, whose *Memoirs of My Nervous Illness* (1903) provided Sigmund Freud with a classic case of paranoid psychosis,[7] suffered from a mental illness that can be profitably analyzed in terms of domination based on a progressive developmental agenda. Schreber's father, the physician Dr. Moritz Schreber, wrote several books on childrearing. He applied his described practices to his own children and recommended them to other parents. Both of his two sons became psychotic, and the older son committed suicide one year before Paul Schreber became institutionalized as a mental patient.

Dr. Schreber advocated total parental control over children. Harsh discipline and complete suppression of the willfulness of the child were used to enforce strict habituation to proper behavior, sentiments, and thoughts. Paradoxically, these childrearing methods were for the sake of the child's moral, mental, and physical health, and ultimately were designed to promote self-determination and free will through the law of habituation to the "Good" and "Right."[8] In other words, they represented a thorough cultural conditioning.

Habituation taught the child the "art of waiting" and the "art of self-denial." The child was mastered, especially by the father, in order to implant "self-determination," "self-reliance," and "free will," by which the child would be "saved" from the "insurmountable enemies of life."[9] The results of these well-meant efforts to produce perfectly successful children were perfect failures, classic examples of the mental illnesses appropriate to a culture of progressive development.

Dr. Schreber believed that training in obedience was a means to a higher end; he advocated that the individual

> strive after full command over thyself, over thy spiritual and bodily weaknesses and wants ... and persevere unweariedly in the struggle for this true (inward) freedom, for the perfection of the self. By this means ... thou shalt go on from victory to victory until thou comest to the final goal with the blissful consciousness that thy life-task has been worthily performed.[10]

Dr. Schreber believed that education should be based on the principle of individualization, and parents should rear their children by acting as living examples and models. Even infants should be optimally stimulated to grow, in part through early training in "moral willpower," "unconscious obedience," and the development of good habits.

Dr. Schreber suffered from a history of depression and advocated using willpower to suppress depressive symptoms and avoid being overwhelmed by them. This idea of self-cure through willpower also influenced his son Paul:

> Endowed with a strong sense of calling and mission, [Dr.] Schreber dreamt of official recognition of his efforts but never received it. This discrepancy between high ambition and insufficient recognition may have contributed to his depressions during the last ten years of his life. The same sense of mission was also discernible in his sons, especially Paul, who doubtless acquired it from their high-striving father. As an adolescent, Paul would have been exposed to his father's depressions, and he would thus have

learned early that long suffering and a lack of recognition may be combined with that inner, almost secret, sense of self-exaltation and higher worth that is the melancholic's chief recompense for his fate.[11]

Paul Schreber was raised as an Evangelical-Lutheran and was trained as a lawyer. Prior to his hospitalization, Paul had suffered a depression, which he described as a "nervous illness" due to mental overstrain, following defeat in an election for the office of judge—a defeat that led to "high sensitivity about frustrated ambitions."[12]   After attaining a new position as a judge, Paul experienced a second illness. Driven to high performance by personal ambition, Paul again overworked. This resulted in a "nervous depression" and a second hospitalization. According to Lothane,

> It was the identification with father's conscientiousness and his ideas about the ethics of love, sex, and work—preached in his books on education and inculcated at home by both parents—that was so crucial in the son's character development and adult conflicts. Paul Schreber grew up to be serious-minded, law-abiding, dutiful and honest to a fault, to the point of a nagging, obsessional ruminativeness. At the height of his career he rebelled; he *refused to perform*. [In addition to depression and survivor guilt,] another prominent motif . . . was the identification with father's quest for fame and a place in history. The streak of ambition runs in the Schreber men from generation to generation, but also the tragic discrepancy between ambition and achievement and the exquisite sensitivity to frustration and rejection.

Paul is identified both with the dream of glory and with the disappointment of failure. He had witnessed the failed ambitions of his father and brother, their trials, despair and rage . . . In his illness he enacted this despair and this rage, theirs and his own. (Author's emphasis.)[13]

Even though a failure as a lawyer and judge, Paul hoped that the *Memoirs* about his illness would provide a legacy comparable to his father's.

Paul Schreber's life and mental illness provide a good example of how seeking leads to relationships of domination and the rebellion against expectations. Paul's rebellion was a manifestation of his shadow-identity, those rejected parts of him that resented the disciplines imposed on him by parental expectations of precocious development—the rejected part of him that wanted instead to relax, stop competing, and enjoy life.

Rather than recognizing the problem and choosing a different lifestyle, Paul could only put an end to his seeking through mental illness, or "nervous exhaustion." For those who are unaware of other options, mental illness may seem the only way out of the dilemma of endless seeking. The common name for this result since the late nineteenth century has been "nervous breakdown."

The suffering caused by seeking and the eventual eruption of the shadow-identity—those rejected parts of the psyche that "refused to perform"—may result in deep depressions, anxiety reactions and panic attacks, numerous physical problems (such as high blood pressure and ulcers), substance abuse, and various other disorders, including psychotic episodes during which one may hear critical, disembodied voices. Paul Schreber experienced most of these symptoms and many more in an unconscious rebellion against the expectations of his father. Although never consciously realized as such, his life and illness became a protest against the progressive developmental agenda that his father had imposed on him.

Chapter 7

Upholding the Ideal

Psychotherapy and the Progressive
Developmental Paradigm

WHEN belief in progressive development is applied to the field of psychology, and especially to the process of therapy, it is assumed to be positive and helpful. The reindoctrination of patients into this paradigm leads to renewed, idealistic goal seeking and expectations of growth, improvement, and positive outcomes. These expectations, however, may be neither realistic nor helpful, especially when they remain unfulfilled through no fault of those involved. Such unfulfilled expectations often lead to negative outcomes, or to a diversion from a reality that needs to be faced as it is, rather than seen as something that must be changed for the better.

Psychotherapists often respond to mental illness with a premature attempt to put Humpty-Dumpty back up on the wall, rather than taking the time to understand why he fell in the first place. Whether the psychotherapist advocates adaptation or growth, he or she does so within a cultural context that determines the disease as much as it determines the treatment. Humpty-Dumpty fell because he was unstable, top-heavy (all head and no body), too high up, and ungrounded. He *needed* to come down from his height—not to be reconstructed as an ambivalent seeker perched on a wall, from which he will inevitably fall again.

125

Modern therapy often attempts to renew the vitality of the seeking self by restoring its progressive development within the contemporary culture. In other words, it determines the good—generally envisioned as cultural adaptation—and evaluates and guides the self in pursuit of a culturally appropriate ideal self-construct. The aim of this culturally-determined treatment, unfortunately, is often the restoration of the underlying condition that led to the illness in the first place. The process of psychotherapy rarely includes a questioning of the cultural context or a thorough investigation of causal connections between the cultural context and the suffering individual. Within the arena of American psychotherapy, the progressive developmental paradigm remains a largely unquestioned value, and its engagement is to be encouraged and restored.

Treating the Symptoms

Much of contemporary mental illness is directly or indirectly related to the naive acceptance of progressive development by individuals who have no alternative perspective. They either fail to perform or succeed. If they succeed, there is no perceived problem; if they fail, they seek help toward ultimate success. Typically, they find themselves caught in a frustrating, life-long process of seeking.

For the therapist, the client's complaint, depression, anxiety, or phobias may appear clear-cut, as an easily diagnosed symptom with a standard treatment solution. Yet for the client, the complaint may unconsciously symbolize an obstacle in his or her broader pursuit of an idealistic agenda. Although poorly defined and with roots in unrealistic parental expectations, rebellious childhood wishes, and early precocious coping responses to trauma, this broader agenda may haunt the individual with an uneasy conscience and lack of self-acceptance.

When these agendas are the hidden cause of observable symptoms, they ought to become the focus of the therapeutic process. But unconscious, idealistic agendas can easily be missed by a treatment that responds only to the surface complaint, by primarily attempting to restore culturally-sanctioned "meanings" and "purposes" in order to resuscitate the seeking self.

This hidden agenda, in fact, is likely to be a cause of the recurrence of specific complaints, and these complaints will continue to recur as long as this broader agenda is pursued. An effective treatment must uncover this underlying agenda, and treat the problem of seeking that is at the root of the superficial symptoms—for example, depression, anxiety, relationship problems—which are so easily identified by both client and therapist.

If the complaint of the individual in psychotherapy can be traced to inappropriate or excessive seeking, and the therapist ignores or fails to recognize the negative influence of seeking in this case, then the client receives, at best, only a band-aid to conceal the problem. This forces the client to continue performing as if there was no option but success, or consequence except failure or madness. Yet this "solution," when successfully implemented, only puts off the problem until the next nervous breakdown, retirement, or death.

Reframing Therapy

Although the goal of progressive development is usually characterized as a form of liberation or fulfillment, the means to this end nearly always involves relationships of domination and servitude. Domination and servitude are inherent in the parent/child relationship, in the relation of the conscience to the seeking self, in the relation of the seeking self to the shadow-identity, and in the relation of the therapist as expert helping the client. If the therapist naturally represents the dominant judging, demanding, or ideal part of the self-construct, there is potentially more to be considered in therapy than the client's superficial complaints.

Therapy provides an opportunity to work on the generic problem of the effects of the progressive developmental paradigm on mental health. This approach would not restore the pursuit of the ideal, but would attempt to provide an opportunity for a complete release from all compulsive striving. This approach would also liberate psychotherapy from its current tendency toward restoring a belief in progressive development, which may itself be a cause of the internal conflict.

Because therapy so easily mirrors a dysfunctional dominant relationship, it also provides an opportunity to unlearn the conditioned pattern of self-dominance, and submission to dominance by others, that is fundamental to seeking. While the therapist may to some degree help the client to cease striving and mourn the lost ideal, this process does not prevent the beginning of another round of striving with similar problems. Such repetitions may be inevitable, but a clearer understanding of the generic problems of the pursuit may lead to better therapeutic outcomes in some cases.

Success in the treatment of specific false beliefs and empty striving is not enough. Successful treatment must address the general problem of seeking, critique the ideologies of progressive development, and recognize the danger that these behaviors and beliefs will inevitably return in other forms. If the client is not prepared to recognize and resist new forms of problematic seeking, he or she will relapse without fail. Habitual submission must give way to rebellion, refusal to perform, and to a true individuality rather than a carbon copy of someone else's.

Psychologist Martin Seligman acknowledges some of the above concerns in his attempt to bring realism to the self-help literature and psychotherapy. He writes that

> improving is absolutely central to American ideology. It is tantamount in importance to freedom in our national identity; indeed, advancement is probably the end for which Americans believe freedom is the means.[1]

While the quest for self-improvement sometimes works,

> distressingly often, self-improvement and psychotherapy fail. The cost is enormous. We think we are worthless. We feel guilty and ashamed. We believe we have no willpower and that we are failures.[2]

Finally, Seligman notes that

> traditionally, most people in the West have believed that human character is fixed and unalterable, that people do not and cannot improve, advance, or perfect themselves. This change from a deep

No, this was a contra in ancient Greek Resurfaced in M.A as Pe

belief in the unchangeability of character to an equally deep belief in the capacity to improve is recent) and it represents one of the most fundamental and important revolutions in modern thought.[3]

This revolution began about three hundred years ago when the restraining influence of religion gradually waned and what is called the "modern self" emerged.

Emergence of the repressed Pagan self

The modern self constructs images of itself as a seeker along with the goals it seeks. It then pursues these imagined goals as "guiding fictions," which are often inappropriately literalized meanings. In other words, fictional goals that are the products of wishful thinking and cultural conditioning are assumed to be real, and the self is believed to be able of achieving them. These goals may then become the substance of a madness that operates by continually mistaking fictional prescriptions and goals for reality. According to James Hillman, these goals, *The shadowside of "heuristic fictions"*

especially the highest and finest, work like overvalued ideas, the roots of delusions that nourish great canopies of sheltering para-noia, those spreading ideals of size and import which characterize the positive goals of so many schools of therapy today . . . we are healed of that goal when we recognize it as a fiction . . . So the best psychotherapy can do is attune the fictional sense. Then the goals toward which therapy strives—maturity, completion, wholeness, actualization—can be seen through as guiding fictions. Therapy becomes less a support of the "great upward drive" than it is a job of deliteralizing the fictions in which purpose is fixed . . .[4]

Hillman is proposing that the self's compulsive tendency

toward striving can be regulated by recognizing the illusory, fictitious nature of the ideals it is striving toward. This is a useful suggestion for psychotherapy, and is a step in the direction of developing a therapeutic approach to the problem of striving in general. The self is intimately bound up with idealistic desires and goal-seeking. Because this is the case, it may experience itself as dependent upon seeking to the extent that the pursuit of ideals is a matter of survival. Alternately, these goals can be appreciated as wishful metaphors that have no bearing on the value or the survival of the self.

On Top of the World

Joe, a thirty-two year old high school dropout, became addicted to drugs as a teenager and spent most of his energy and time buying and using them. Because he started using drugs early, Joe hadn't developed a strong, positive sense of self before he became addicted to the ideal, "high" self he discovered using drugs.

Joe's artificially created ideal self-construct was powerful, confident, and optimistic about his future. When intoxicated and identified with this self-construct, he felt on top of the world, able to master any situation, and assured that he would succeed in any endeavor. But each "high" lasted less than an hour, followed by a fall down a slippery slope into the depths of depression and frustration. He sought to return to and maintain his ideal "high" self-construct as often and for as long as he could. The powerful psychological portion of his addiction was the desire to return to his "high" self-construct and avoid his "straight self," and almost all of his energy was focused on this pursuit.

Because of growing physical tolerance, Joe's addiction became more difficult to maintain. Each high resulted in diminishing returns and the aftereffects became more burdensome. It wasn't until he was arrested and imprisoned that he was able to detoxify himself and acknowledge the futility of his quest to remain high. Finally, Joe recognized the price he paid for getting high: daily work only to obtain money for drugs; the legal risk of purchase and use; and most importantly, the aftereffects: coming down, hangover, intolerance of sobriety and of his normal "straight self," damage to relationships and commitments, and general psychological instability due to the mood swings he experienced daily.

In prison with the help of group therapy, Joe recognized that returning to his high self-construct was futile and not worth the price. Although drugs gave him a glimpse of what seemed to be a desirable self, a self he could love, he recognized that is all they would ever be able to do for him. To spend five percent of his time enjoying this glimpse and relief from the shame of his ordinary self, and ninety-five percent of his time striving to return to this artificial, ideal self, was ultimately a nightmare, not the fulfillment of his narcissistic dreams. He finally gave up seeking new highs in favor of enjoying the ordinary pleasures of life, which he learned to appreciate in a way he had not been able to before.

Summary

The following points are made in this chapter:

1. Progressive developmental beliefs in therapy are questionable since they tend to produce unrealistic expectations, defensiveness, the concealment of faults, and ultimately a renewal of the symptoms that led to treatment.

2. If therapy supports the progressive developmental paradigm and the beginning of a new round of seeking, it has treated the symptom, not the disease.

3. Therapy provides an opportunity to work on the problem of seeking, but only if it recognizes the underlying cause, avoids supporting renewed striving, and focuses on the problem of self-domination and domination by others shaped by ideal cultural expectations.

4. Recognizing the fictional nature of the goals of striving may help reduce the overvaluation of striving.

[handwritten annotation at top: I also speculated in REE that the mental-ration structure could be a Reaction formation, but to literalize this as RL may, subjects him to the pre/tron fallacy]

Historical Example 3: Holy Anorexia—
A Study of Self-Destruction

MENTAL ILLNESSES associated with the progressive developmental paradigm have occurred throughout recorded history. This history can be traced, for example, through the Old Testament in the convergence and parallel development of monotheism, individuality, and selfhood, based on the internalization of ethical rules and the beginnings of a progressive developmental interpretation of history. The dualistic and otherworldly emphasis of Platonism eventually undermined the message of Greek tragedy, that seeking to determine one's fate was impious and would be punished by the gods. Inheriting these and other strands of tradition, Christianity was very ambivalent in its critique of spiritual striving, and few ordinary believers understood why a critique was even attempted.

The history of all cultures, both East and West, shows the gradual appearance of progressive developmental tendencies, culminating in the modern era. But in the West, and particularly in American culture, these tendencies are most strongly manifested. For example, Americans suffer much more severely from them than do Indian, Russian, or Chinese individuals.

[handwritten margin note: In America it's hyperbolic whereas Europe is more grounded historically]

In the different historical periods of Western culture, the mental illnesses associated with the progressive developmental paradigm have adapted to different cultural goals, but have nevertheless followed a similar pattern. The history of sainthood in Christianity provides numerous case studies of severe and chronic suffering due to spiritual striving. These cases also provide ex-

[handwritten annotation at bottom: yes, but let's not forget the stultifying complacency of premodern & prerational cultures]

amples of how extreme the self-sacrifice and consequences of seeking must be, at least for some individuals, before involuntary transformation occurs.

In the Middle Ages, the primary goal for seekers was spirituality, whereas in the modern era the goal is often more concrete and external (for example, improving one's appearance). But regardless of the goal, identity may become dependent upon seeking to the point where the behaviors associated with seeking become more important than life itself.

The word *anorexia* refers to any significant reduction of appetite or dislike of food. Although "anorexia nervosa," the illness that will be described below, has a long history in Western culture, it was not understood as a separate illness until 1868, when William Gull described a strange malady of young women who refused to eat even as they became extremely thin. Symptoms included extreme weight loss, lack of menstruation, and hyperactivity. Recent descriptions of the illness include the following by Hilde Bruch:

> Anorexics struggle against feeling enslaved, exploited, and not permitted to lead a life of their own. They would rather starve than continue a life of accommodation. In this blind search for a sense of identity and selfhood they will not accept anything that their parents, or the world around them, has to offer . . . the main theme is a struggle for control, for a sense of identity, competence, and effectiveness.[5]

Anorexia provides the means, the progressive developmental

discipline, for establishing an identity, in this case through a form of asceticism:

> the preanorexic may see the shaping of her body as the "first possible move in defining the dimensions (literally) of what one will be" . . . It is the most accessible territory that can be conquered by the self—and may be one of the few aspects of life over which it is really possible to obtain the "absolute control" or contemplate the "total success" that . . . anorexics crave. The choice of dieting as a vehicle for self-improvement is further strengthened by the association between self-deprivation and self-control, which possess their own intrinsic value for these ascetic individuals.[6]

Weight loss becomes a moral quest through starvation; it combines an increasing sense of identity and power with the spiritual purity and physical attractiveness that seem guaranteed to win the approval of others. Refusing food becomes a disciplined process of ascetic seeking, around which an identity forms and strengthens itself—an identity that believes itself in control of its destiny.

The father of the anorexic is typically a driving, ambitious, upwardly mobile individual who is opinionated, controlling, and demanding. The anorexic is an overachiever who strives for perfection in order to become lovable to her selfish parents and others; this is a compensatory reaction to underlying profound feelings of unlovability, inferiority, and powerlessness. She is sensitive to the expectations and negative judgments of others, and molds herself accordingly:

"if the problem consists of drawing a sense of self out of others' judgments, perfectionism logically becomes the way to provide a positive solution to the problem." If one can avoid committing any errors, consistently anticipating, fulfilling, and even surpassing the expectations of the audience, one may both avoid censure and secure reassurance about one's basic worth.[7]

The anorexic becomes trapped in seeking perfection of appearance, but over time begins to feel like an impersonator or imposter. That is because she recognizes her continued imperfection at the same time she secretly believes in fantasies of great success, of becoming one of the "beautiful people," a model or celebrity loved by everyone. Fear of being discovered to be imperfect adds to a strong motivation to continue dieting, whatever the cost. The discipline of dieting becomes an essential survival tool of the self.

Anorexia can be associated with progressive development due to its pursuit of an ideal bodily appearance. This pursuit gains a life of its own, as it becomes nearly impossible for the anorexic to accept her achievement of an ideal body weight and stop dieting. Due to starvation, anorexia has the highest mortality rate of any psychiatric disorder. The features associated with this mental illness include the pursuit of an unachievable ideal, an inability to even temporarily stop the pursuit, and the tendency of the pursuit to be a flight from internal and external negative circumstances.

In addition to being a struggle for identity through pursuit of the perfectly thin body, anorexia is sometimes a rebellion against cultural prescriptions. The anorexic may be rebelling against the anticipated consequences of growing up, such as marriage, sexual intercourse, motherhood, the woman's role in culture, and the responsibilities of adulthood. Alternately, the self-imposed discipline of anorexia is also a means of individuation, a way of gaining power and control over one's life, of taking responsibility, a way of maturing (in the sense of assuming self-control), and a way of fulfilling the assumed expectations of others.

In contrast to the cultural framework of the modern anorexic, there is a history of anorexia among women in medieval Europe oriented around the pursuit of salvation. These women have been described as suffering from "holy anorexia" by Rudolph Bell. The holy anorexic, he writes, "emerges from a frightened, insecure, psychic world superficially veiled by her outwardly pleasant disposition to become a champion in the race for (bodily/spiritual) perfection."[8]

In medieval times, it was possible to achieve success as an anorexic if the behavior was seen as spiritual, in which case the anorexic became an object of awe and reverence, admired for her heroism and denial of self and bodily desires. However, this determination had to be made by skeptical male clerics, which sometimes resulted in charges of heresy and witchcraft. But if the behavior was determined to be saintly rather than demonic or sick, the woman would be judged to have found her calling and vocation, in addition to establishing a spiritual identity based on anorexic behaviors.

One example of this outcome is that of Saint Catherine of Siena, who lived in the late fourteenth century, and by the age of twenty-six had already become well-known for holiness and extreme fasting. She reported that she followed the dictates of her bridegroom, Jesus Christ, and refused to follow the directions of her confessors—all men—who ordered her to eat. Her male confessors were assigned to watch, control, and guide her in the path to holiness, as well as protect the Church from a possible heretic; but she was cleared by a formal Church commission, and her behavior was judged to be spiritually motivated.

Realizing that her fasting and self-punishment did not in themselves bring her closer to spiritual perfection, Catherine "urged 'holy hatred' of oneself [and believed that] the essential effort had to be the destruction of self-will, not the accumulation of superficially meritorious acts."[9] She eventually developed a following, attempted to reform the Church, and tried to establish a community for those seeking religious perfection, but starved herself to death when it became clear that her efforts were unsuccessful.

Catherine grew up in a world where the standard path to adulthood for women was the transition from parental domination to submission before a husband in an arranged marriage. Catherine was rebellious and wanted to establish an identity of her own, but there were no culturally accepted routes for women to pursue independence except through spirituality. The pattern of "recovered" holy anorexics during this period of history is summarized by Bell as follows:

a superficially obedient but deeply strong-willed child is brought up in great religiosity, usually by her mother; in her early teens her father takes over and presses her to marry; she resists and comes to display the classic anorexic syndrome; ultimately she runs away to a convent; during her novitiate and for several years thereafter, she is deeply depressed, tormented by demonic visions, and still unable to eat; gradually, usually in her late twenties or early thirties, she "recovers" and becomes active in the affairs of the convent . . . [and] learns to fast rigorously but in a fully self-controlled way . . .[10]

For the holy anorexic, possession by God was the solution to the earthly obstacles to achieving independence, resulting in a liberation from family, confessors, and anyone who would attempt to control her life. This path also avoided the fate of being married and having to submit to sexuality and motherhood. It also countered the general Christian consensus that condemned women to subordinate spiritual roles. To marry and engage in sexual intercourse added to the spiritual uncleanliness already associated with women, since women—due to misogyny and projection of male desire—were considered a danger to male salvation, and unable to relate to God. According to the Church, virginity and purity were necessary prerequisites for women to establish a relationship with God. The body was corrupt, an obstacle to salvation, and salvation required freedom from the shackles of sexual desire and hunger.

The holy anorexic rebelled against the passive and dependent Christianity she was offered by its male priesthood, seeking instead an intimate union with God. Once she felt this had been achieved, her defiance was justified by the authority of her recognized spirituality; in her mind, the male power structure, both secular and religious, had lost its control over her. She now felt in a position of strength and independence, as though her will were God's will.

The anorexic ideal spread geographically and continued to be a prominent model through the fourteenth and fifteenth centuries:

Nearly half of the forty-two Italian women who lived and died in the thirteenth century and who came to be recognized as saints exhibited an anorexic behavior pattern. Thus a new ideal of female piety was forged . . . In this quest their bodies became impediments, painful reminders of the earthly realities they sought to transcend.[11]

With the Reformation in the sixteenth century, fear of and prejudice against women by the Protestant ecclesiastical male hierarchy increased, and the charge of heresy was more common. Female spirituality came to be seen as insane or demoniacal, and the male priesthood jealously guarded its religious control.

Eventually, these anorexic, spiritual women began to be regarded as ill, subjects for medical examination. While occasionally recognized as holy sufferers, they were finally only discussed in medical textbooks, and anorexia was rediscovered as a medical diagnosis in the late nineteenth century.

During medieval times, progressive development came at a price, as spirituality was typically gained through long and severe suffering, if at all. Self-sacrificial suffering was saintly, and the extreme ascetic was a spiritual hero or heroine. Even from the modern perspective, holy anorexia is praiseworthy as a heroic rebellion, and, at times apparently a successful method to achieve a traditional, ascetic type of Christian spirituality.

Both in medieval Italy and modern-day America, anorexics are hyperactive, perfectionistic, never satisfied with their fanatical efforts to become holy or thin, self-critical, and paranoid about maintaining control of their agendas. They are typically repulsed by sexuality and selfishness, and are obsessed with mental and physical purity. Anorexic women usually see themselves as extremely self-sufficient and independent, as long as they are in control of their self-sacrificial agenda. Without it, they lose their sense of self and fall into a depression.

The concern here is not about whether the path of anorexic seeking was successful, but about its excessiveness, fanaticism, and self-destructiveness. The holy anorexic and modern anorexic both provide an example of how driven such quests for identity and spirituality can become, especially when they seem as if they are the only way out of a difficult situation. But is such drivenness necessary, or is it an overreaction that is often more harmful than helpful? The harm of this quest becomes apparent in the modern version of anorexia, where the drive for an acceptable appearance often results in unacceptability—thinness to the point of ugliness—and may have been intended to do so in the first place, through fear of intimacy and sexuality. The harm is also apparent in the high rate of death of those taking this path.

There were and are successful anorexics, both in medieval times and the present, but they are a small minority whose success obscures the majority, who fail and suffer miserably from perfectionistic seeking. The distortions of perception and extremities of behavior in anorexics suggest an unconscious attempt to remove themselves from the normal course of development. This represents an unconscious rebellion of the shadow-identity transformed into a quest for perfection or a spiritual agenda.

This interpretation helps explain why many of these women, in both Catholic and later Protestant contexts, were accused of witchcraft, since they followed the dictates of their rebellious and—to the male hierarchy—devilish inclinations.[12] Deprived of any path to independence, they resorted to nature worship, pagan ritual, and even devotion to Satan, as the archetypal enemy of their patriarchal oppressors. Since their religion had failed them, many felt that they had no alternative but to seek solace, healing, and understanding in the shadow-side of their culture, which seemed to be the only place where they could find real power to change their lives.

In the modern form of anorexia, a progressive developmental prescription—the pursuit of the ideal body shape—becomes distorted and fanaticized to the point that the individual becomes enslaved to the prescription. The prescription can neither be realized nor given up since the identity created by this process requires a repetition of associated rituals for its psychological survival. The mind rules the objectified, disconnected body, and manipulates it according to its selfish needs, rather than honoring the needs of the body. Rather than being experienced and inhabited, the body is used and abused in the service of a self-serving agenda.

Identities formed through performance of progressive developmental prescriptions are often impossible to release, since those who follow the regimens feel threatened by the possibility of an end of striving. The self-construct that is created and maintained by this striving depends upon continued striving, even if it leads to death. For the anorexic, giving up the quest would result in an immediate, psychological death; but to die in its performance is a demonstration of loyalty to one's cause, and a postponement of death until the body gives out, rather than an immediate death of the heroic self-construct. Just as Catherine of Siena became a martyr to her cause, so many modern anorexics become martyrs to their progressive developmental agendas.

Wisdom Sample 7

IF THERE is one religion where the critique of seeking spirituality is a central issue, it is Islam. *Islam* means submission to the will of God, and the *Muslim* is one who has submitted to the will of God. Understanding the will of God is based on the recital (*Koran*) of God's messenger, the prophet Mohammed, during the years 610 to 632 C.E. Islamic law, or the *Shari'a*, a model of a more or less unattainable ideal, provides guidance as to what the Muslim should and should not do, based on the *Koran*. Spiritual guidance is supplemented by the sayings of the Prophet (*hadith*), his behavior, and the behavior of his family and community in Medina and Mecca during his lifetime.

It is the personal obligation of every Muslim to fully obey Islamic law. This unceasing struggle or *jihad* is recorded, and will be evaluated by God at the final judgment. God is merciful and the individual is not expected to achieve perfection, but the Muslim must make every reasonable effort to understand and obey the will of God. Paradoxically, in this context where submission is the focus, there is little argument about *whether* one should seek, only about *how* one should seek.

The Muslim, like the Christian, is encouraged to seek spirituality through obeying the word and guidance of God, but for the Muslim there is less room for individual initiative, so the problem of striving is limited to assessing the degree of obedience to Islamic law. The Muslim would say that this problem of religious striving only arises in Christianity and other Western religions because of ignorance and doubt, the lack of a complete revelation of God's will, and doubt about the meaning of what has been revealed. Since the *Koran* and the other Islamic literature claims to contain all that can and should be known about God's will, the only question that arises about the individual will of the Muslim is concerns knowledge of, and obedience to, God's will.

Islamic mysticism is called *Sufism* and is aimed at attaining an intense emotional comprehension of God's being. As a religion of the heart, Sufism provides acute insights into, and criticisms of, those religious institutions that support self-appointed authorities and pretenders to religious knowledge. Rabia al-Adawiyya (717–801) was one of the first in the Sufi tradition. She proclaimed that affirmation of unity required absolute acceptance of divine will. Absolute acceptance was active, and led to an authentic life—not to passivity or fatalism. Rabia criticized Islamic authorities for becoming attached to their religious rituals, treating them as an end in themselves. According to Rabia, to ask anything of God was to betray one's acceptance of divine will. Thus, sincerity in the spiritual quest was incompatible with acting out of hope for reward or fear of punishment. To put one's trust in one's own plan was to make a god of that plan.

Active acceptance was absolute acceptance of the infinite divine will, as nothing happened without the will of all-powerful God. The ultimate spiritual goal was extinction of the ego-self in union with the Divine Beloved, following which God worked in and through the human.

The Sufis, much like those in the Christian mystical tradition, claimed that all ways to God required the annihilation of the self, that love came from self-denial, and that a sense of justice was only possible if the mind had rid itself of selfishness and arrogance. A story from an early Sufi illustrates the obstacle of the self on the quest:

> Shibli was asked: "Who guided you in the Path?" He said: "A dog. One day I saw him, almost dead with thirst, standing by the water's edge. Every time he looked at his reflection in the water he was frightened and withdrew, because he thought it was another dog. Finally, such was his necessity, he cast away fear and leapt into the water, at which the 'other dog' vanished. The dog found that the obstacle, which was himself, the barrier between him and what he sought, melted away. In this same way my own obstacle vanished, when I knew that it was what I took to be my own self. And my Way was first shown to me by the behavior of a dog."[13]

Sufism is a religion of the heart and of seeking the Beloved. Seeking the Beloved is not the same as seeking the ideal. To become the ideal is a roundabout way of soliciting the Beloved by becoming lovable, but Sufis ignore this diversion in favor of a direct approach. More than trusting and depending upon the other, Sufism advocates becoming the other in a fusion of love. For example, Ibn 'Arabi (1165–1240) described Sufism as an intimate sharing between God and the mystic: "If He has given us life and existence by His being, I also give Him life by knowing Him in my heart."[14] Once this knowing is attained, one is no longer threatened by one's reflection in the water. Love melts away the obstacles of the taskmaster conscience and the heroic seeker, and life becomes a celebrative revelation of the reunion of the soul.

Chapter 8

The Challenge of Integration

THINKING is often a reaction to a problem, and the intent of such thought is to resolve the problem through self-initiated change. This creates a tension between what one desires—the imagined solution—and what is. But when this intention to initiate change is directed at the self, suffering results due to lack of self-acceptance, unproductive agitation towards change, and the splitting of the self into conflicting parts.

The tendency to engage in agendas for change reflects a lack of acceptance of what is, especially of the self, its inevitable inadequacies, and imperfections. Yet as many wise individuals have reminded their contemporaries throughout history, to be human is to be imperfect. It is better to remain human and imperfect than to attempt the impossible task of becoming perfect—that is, of becoming divine, and, therefore, inhuman. Acceptance, or at least tolerance, of the imperfect self is preferable to suffering from self-inflicted wounds. A discipline of acceptance, in the long run, is more desirable and effective than the frustrating and ultimately impossible agenda of attempting to become what one is not.

It is the culturally conditioned reaction to difficulties—blaming the self and trying to improve it, not the difficulties themselves—that becomes the primary problem, the cause of the disintegration of the self. These conditioned tendencies toward the creation of self-improvement agendas are encouraged by the many predatory peddlers of instant solutions, which includes much of the self-help and "metaphysical" literature, where promises are made to fulfill nearly any desire, provided there is a willingness to believe in, practice, and pay for a spiritual product and discipline.

Thus, willful effort toward radical self-improvement is a source of suffering. The self formed around this effort has a tendency to create and strengthen the separation and conflict between the self, conscience, ideal self-construct, and the shadow-identity. The goals of this striving are all too often misinformed illusions of what is desirable, and of how one becomes desirable and loved, and are based on unrealistic models provided by the culture. But it is not in the interest of the striving self to entirely succeed or entirely fail, as both of these outcomes threaten its very existence as a harried self-construct on a quest.

The result is a ghost-like self-construct, an insubstantial, disembodied wraith, living in an imaginary world. This ghost haunts itself and others with the residue of generations of unfinished business. Unable to rest in peace, it lives in a hell of its own making. Trapped in a waking nightmare, this ghost-self finds itself in an endless chain of negative self-judgments and self-imposed tasks that keep it in a state of constant agitation and conflict. This is a nightmare from which the benighted self cannot wake up. Waking up would require the recognition that existence and self-acceptance is not dependent upon performance, and that it is, after all, possible to awaken into the sensible world, which remains after illusions disappear.

The suggested alternative to this nightmare—the end of self-interested seeking—is not a prescription for detachment from life, for the avoidance of effort, emotional sensitivity, or for distancing oneself from the difficulties of life. It is, rather, a recommendation for removing one of the primary obstacles to the enjoyment of life, and encourages engaging *in* life rather than in an illusory and self-destructive imitation *of* life. Although the emotions associated with engagement in progressive developmental processes have come to be identified with life itself, other emotions that are equally if not more vital can be experienced when self-interested striving is completely absent. The resulting discovery is a new form of experience, a self-love so rare—and so different from the narcissism of the seeking self—that it may be incorrectly interpreted in religious terms as a "revelation," a rebirth, or a gift from God. But integration is simply a return to the natural unitary experience of childhood, experienced in mature form, that was lost in the struggle to conform and perform. — ? or *p* +f ?

Without a supporting tradition of thought, the individual who would wake up from this nightmare is required to independently achieve a radical discovery. But this discovery of a mysterious integration that breaches current cultural and ethical boundaries is extremely rare. That is because there is no generally available guidance, encouragement, or confirmation of this goal to facilitate the recognition of its possibility. *except Lord, of course.*

On the other hand, once integration is experienced, the lack of a contemporary critical tradition of thought about seeking leaves little alternative but to distort this experience by interpreting it as *+ not to do to is to distort* the product of one's personal quest, as a religious revelation, or as the product of traditional or cult disciplines. Paradoxically, the dissemination of these distortions then tends to encourage further errant seeking by others, and supports the progressive developmental culture that prevents natural integrative experiences from occurring.

It remains to be seen whether a treatment of problematic seeking can be developed that will go beyond an intellectual grappling with this problem. The treatment of specific illusory goals is one thing, but the treatment of the problem of seeking in general is a therapeutic skill that has yet to be developed. To remove a particular belief and stop a particular type of seeking is a necessary first step, but does not constitute a cure. Success in confronting a particular belief is likely to be interpreted as a success of seeking, in which case the progressive developmental paradigm will be redeemed by its assumed role in creating that success, and no fundamental challenge will have been offered to it.

Culturally constructed perspectives are the lens through which all individuals view and understand the world. Since most Western individuals have grown up in a modernist culture that emphasizes the progressive developmental paradigm, they see and understand the world through the lens of this paradigm. The self-contained individual can only be known to itself through its beliefs *about* itself rather than as a thing *in* itself. This is another reason why it is crucial to create a critical tradition that will provide the modern self with a different perspective for understanding itself and an alternate set of options for being and becoming.

It would seem that understanding and agreement with the point of view explored in this book is rare in Western culture. The only consistent advice supporting this point of view comes from some pre-Christian philosophers, a relatively obscure and ambivalent tradition in Christianity, and from some Eastern philosophers and religions. But these sources are not compelling, either because of their dated, doctrinal focus, or because they come from a different historical and cultural context. I have nevertheless summarized them in more detail in another book, *The Devil's Due*.

For a credible alternative to seeking to become available, a Western tradition of thought will have to be created that is culturally and historically relevant for contemporary individuals—one that is able to provide an authoritative alternative to the progressive developmental paradigm. To my knowledge, there is no such current tradition, but the likely place to begin to establish a critical perspective is in the field of psychology. In psychology, the self-destructive consequences of the progressive developmental paradigm can be explored and documented, and effective treatment approaches can be identified and honed.

If, as I believe, there is a cultural shift in the not too distant future away from the progressive developmental paradigm, the need for a therapeutic approach may become even more compelling. Alternately, the continuing overuse and exploitation of this paradigm by various media will lead to more frequent crises of conscience, "nervous breakdowns," and an increased need for treatment. In either case, in modern Western culture the field of psychology will most likely bear the responsibility for providing understanding and treatment for the victims of this ideology, or for failing to do so.

Any therapist who has read this book should be able to easily identify several examples from experience where, behind the initial complaint, the client's pursuit of an ideal was the fundamental problem. On the surface it may seem that most of these clients will be found among the "worried well"; but a deeper look would reveal that no group is exempt, and that each has distinctive variations on progressive developmental themes. Given our pervasive conditioning, how could it be otherwise? Even the desire to be "normal" or to have a "strong self" can be a dysfunctional, progressive developmental agenda.

Life Beyond Striving

The child seeks to become an adult. The adult seeks to maintain a youthful appearance. Among the poor, the American Dream is a very compelling yet unreachable goal that is pursued by purchasing the lucky winning lottery ticket. The middle class seek to become wealthy. The wealthy seek to be recognized as valuable apart from their wealth; the famous apart from what they are famous for. The discontented and disillusioned are conditioned to seek self-realization or transcendence. The mentally ill seek to become normal, and the normal seek to be uniquely different, "above the norm."

Although many people seem to reach the end of their rope in pursuit of ideals, they do not recognize the alternative of giving up seeking altogether. This is because, after creating and structuring a self-construct based on the progressive developmental paradigm, to give it up is experienced as mental illness or psychological death. Despite some Western and Eastern recommendations in favor of the death of the self, no one seems willing to take this leap, which would be unwise, in any case, without further guidance.

The "death of the self," referred to in transformative experiences, means that the striving that formerly sustained the self ends. This striving ends involuntarily, not by choice, and the self-construct formed by this effort naturally ends with it. The ideal self-construct dissipates into thin air, the shadow-identity is reintegrated, and the former divisiveness is replaced by a new state of consciousness that is no longer in conflict with itself. The release of energy, the expansion of awareness into body and world, and the emergence of a new perspective on experience that results from this reintegration has often been named "grace" or "enlighten-ment."

The old, striving self "dies," but remains functional and is not replaced by a new self-construct based on striving, even though life goes on and various agendas and projects continue to occupy the individual. The integrated psyche is no longer driven by personal and cultural agendas. The conscience dissolves in compassionate participation in the world, and what is left of the "self" is now radically free to enjoy itself as it is, warts and all.

The reason this outcome is relatively rare is that, from the point of view of the individual, such an involuntary letting go of what sustains the self would have to be the result of a genuine, sincere, and long-lasting struggle. Most individuals either manage to avoid this depth of engagement or reach a state of paralytic withdrawal, wherein they fear to continue, but refuse to let go or recognize defeat. Although they are aware that continuation of the struggle to change oneself for the better is counterproductive, they cannot completely accept what appears to be an even worse alternative of acknowledging their helplessness and inability to reach personal, ideal goals. *Woe to you, O sinners!*

In the rare case of a full recognition of the futility of striving, there may be readiness for an alternative. But because there is no consistent guidance about this dilemma, unless a spontaneous transformation occurs, any movement toward integration may require a long period of gestation and probably need some help along the way. Apart from the intellectual understanding of its

Just say no!
Become a non-seeker!

AA straight

futility, a strong distaste for striving would be required to make the ex-seeker avoid further bouts of seeking / *alcohol / drugs etc*

People at this point might be advised to find a Western therapist or mentor who could help them through a difficult period of adjustment to this realization, which might include a mourning of the loss of former ideals. However, these therapists are very rare, and their techniques unproven because they are largely unused. Apart from such an exceptional mentor or therapist, if any can be found, the individual is on his or her own in this process.

It can also be helpful to at least find written confirmation in a book about this apparently new point of view, and to realize that the revelation of powerlessness is not a tragedy, but an opportunity to end the struggles and suffering associated with a life of futile pursuits. It may also be important and helpful to recognize that one is not alone in this point of view.

There is some literature available that is supportive of this realization, usually claiming to be influenced by Zen teachings, or other Eastern religious points of view. These can be helpful, but they usually do not provide the kind of explanation Westerners require for even a superficial understanding of these topics, since they only mention relevant dilemmas in passing and fail to fully explore their implications in the Western cultural context. As a result, their brief references to non-attachment and the removal or death of the self remain obscure, if not incomprehensible, to the average Western reader. One notable exception is Steven Harrison's book *Doing Nothing: Coming to the End of the Spiritual Search*, where realization of the futility of seeking is described in personal, graphic, and convincing language. Another book is Byron Brown's *Soul without Shame: A Guide to Liberating Yourself from the Judge*

Within, which suggests techniques that may prove useful for undermining the taskmaster conscience.

In the East, as in the West, during the historical period when most of the currently available recommendations to give up seeking were originally made, only the philosophical and religious contexts existed in which to understand them. But in the current Western context, the situation is different. The progressive developmental paradigm is currently decentered, seeming to appear everywhere, yet united by the promotion of self-interested striving, and based on promises with idealistic, if not religious, implications. The cultural context in which this paradigm is promoted is therefore complex, multileveled, and intimately bound up with personal identity and its maintenance. This complexity, and the countercultural nature of the opposing point of view, requires more clarification in the current Western context than may have been necessary in the past.

From a modern American point of view, what I am suggesting should seem vaguely if not explicitly unethical, or at least amoral. It is likely to be seen as a threat to the fabric of society and sense of community, potentially leading to anarchy and regression into primitive chaos. But it is precisely the civilized ethics that promote this fear that are responsible for the majority of those aberrant behaviors that are incorrectly assumed to be natural or inherent. Civilized ethics justify repressive moral systems whose consequences then create a vicious cycle of further aberrant behaviors justifying their existence.

If integrated psyches were the norm, empathy and compassion for others would tend to shape behavior in such a way that current ethical ideals would naturally be achieved and surpassed. Individuals in empathic and intuitive communion with each other would be less likely to harm each other because it would be nearly the same thing as harming themselves. But the problem of attempting to create such a utopia even in a small community—and its unlikelihood any time soon—must give one pause.

It is difficult to maintain a rational discourse about experiences that are outside the range of current language. The inscrutable nature of these realizations is evident in the enigmatic discourse of the Zen master with the seeker of enlightenment. Rational discourse is insufficient for communication designed to bring about attainment of integration, or to answer the "how-to" question most often posed by the seeker. In fact, the "how-to" question is usually a symptom of the problem.

It may not, after all, be a question of finding an *answer*, but rather the challenge of seeing the problem of self-destructive seeking, taking it seriously, and struggling to come to terms with it. The majority of the work, if not all of it, has to be done by the individual based on his or her experience. One must first understand that a problem exists and then determine what the problem consists of. What to do about it is to understand it, objectify it, and stop participating in it in self-destructive ways.

A dialogue with someone who also understands this would be helpful, especially in the beginning. If this dialogue moved in the direction of an educational approach to treatment, it might, for example, consist of questions designed to expose the various assumptions underlying the identity of the heroic seeker. Questions could be raised such as: What are you seeking?, How are you seeking it?, and How are you going to achieve this goal? How much progress have you made? Why are you suffering? Who are you? Why don't you like yourself as you are? What would it be like if you achieved your goal?

These open-ended questions, comparable to unanswerable Zen koans, would provoke a thorough questioning and understanding of the general context of the modern, heroic, seeking self-construct. Of course, as a Zen master might comment, attempting to answer these questions is part of the problem, but failing in these attempts, and finally realizing that many of these questions have no satisfactory answers, may open one's eyes a little wider.

There are no answers, no alternatives, but simply the inevitably altered lifestyle that may result from a change of attitude and disengagement from self-interested striving, whether through integration or through a determination to end unnecessary suffering. For some this may be a revolutionary change, for others a minor adjustment, and for some not worthy of serious consideration.

As much as I have tried to demystify the goals and consequences of seeking, reintegration remains a mysterious event that happens, or does not happen, according to its own rules. Recognizing that self-interested seeking is unproductive is a first step, but the last step comes with a will of its own.

Notes

Introduction

1. For Eastern cultures, see McGreal 1995; for Western cultures, see Boorstin 1998, Lind 1999, and Taylor 1989; for American culture, see Bellah, et al. 1986, Lesser 1999, and Roof 1999.

2. Ramaswami and Sheikh 1989, 90.

3. Epstein 1995, 72.

4. Johansson 1969, 10.

5. Johansson 1969, 22, 114, 69.

Chapter One

1. Lattimore 1960, 28.

2. Lattimore 1960, 55–56.

3. Tuan 1998.

4. Rohde 1966.

5. Lind 1999, 99.

6. Bloom 1986, 101–5.

7. Mair 1990, 142–43.

8. Lao Tzu 1992, x–xi.

9. Lao Tzu 1992, xi–xii.

10. Lao Tzu 1992, xiii.

11. Lao Tzu 1992, xiii.

12. Lao Tzu 1990, 60.

13. Lao Tzu 1990, 34.

14. Lao Tzu 1990, 86.

Chapter Two

1. Jung 1959.
2. Nussbaum 1986, 78.

Chapter Three

1. Nussbaum 1994, 105.
2. Lucretius, quoted in Nussbaum 1994, 197–98.

Chapter Four

1. Dabrowski 1964, 22.
2. Dabrowski 1964, 5–6.
3. Dabrowski 1964, 13, 95.
4. Dabrowski 1964, 63.
5. Kohut 1977 and 1984.
6. Friedman 1980, 416.
7. Friedman 1980, 413.
8. Hoover 1977, 3–4.
9. Hendricks 1998, 20.
10. D. Suzuki, quoted in Faure 1993, 6.

Chapter Five

1. O'Hear 1999.
2. Lind 1999.
3. Cushman 1990.
4. Rose 1990, 11.
5. Bunyan, *Grace Abounding*, in Clebsh and Jaekle 1983, 275–76.
6. Luther 1957, 268.

7. Wesley 1960, 22.

Chapter Six

1. Singer and Salovey 1993, 80.

2. Golomb 1992, 12.

3. Golomb 1992, 28.

4. Golomb 1992, 29.

5. Golomb 1992, 20.

6. Golomb 1992, 157.

7. See Freud 1993.

8. Schatzman 1971.

9. Schatzman 1971, 191–93.

10. Dr. Schreber, quoted in Lothane 1992, 163–64.

11. Lothane 1992, 121.

12. Lothane 1992, 33.

13. Lothane 1992, 447.

Chapter Seven

1. Seligman 1993, 16.

2. Seligman 1993, 3.

3. Seligman 1993, 17.

4. Hillman 1983, 105.

5. Bruch 1978, 250–51.

6. Vitousek and Ewald 1993, 232.

7. Guidano, quoted in Vitousek and Ewald 1993, 226.

8. Bell 1985, 20.

9. Bell 1985, 28.

10. Bell 1985, 56.

11. Bell 1985, 149.

12. For the Catholic context, see Cervantes 1994; for the Protestant context, see Hall 1989.

13. Arasteh and Sheikh 1989, 146.

14. Quoted in Corbin 1969, 247.

Bibliography

Arasteh, A., and A. Sheikh. 1989. Sufism: The way to universal self. In *Healing East and West: Ancient wisdom and modern psychology*, edited by A. Sheikh and K. Sheikh. New York: John Wiley.

Barratt, B. 1984. *Psychic reality and psychoanalytic knowing*. Hillsdale: Analytic Press.

Bell, R. 1985. *Holy anorexia*. Chicago: University of Chicago Press.

Bellah, R., R. Madsen, W. Sullivan, A. Swidler, and S. Tipton. 1986. *Habits of the heart: Individualism and commitment in American life*. New York: Harper & Row.

Bloom, A. 1986. The Song of the Nembutsu. In *Shoshinge: The heart of Shin Buddhism*. Honolulu: Buddhist Study Center Press.

Boorstin, D. 1998. *The seekers: The story of man's continuing quest to understand his world*. New York: Random House.

Brown, B. 1999. *Soul without shame: A guide to liberating yourself from the judge within*. Boston: Shambhala.

Bruch, H. 1978. *The golden cage: The enigma of anorexia nervosa*. Cambridge: Cambridge University Press.

Cervantes, F. 1994. *The devil in the New World: The impact of diabolism in New Spain*. New Haven: Yale University Press.

Clebsh, W., and C. Jaekle. 1983. *Pastoral care in historical perspective*. Northvale: Jason Aronson.

Corbin, H. 1969. *Creative imagination in the Sufism of Ibn 'Arabi*.

Princeton: Princeton University Press.

Cushman, P. 1990. Why the self is empty: Toward a historically situated psychology. *American Psychologist* 45:599–611.

Dabrowski, K. 1964. *Positive disintegration*. Boston: Little Brown.

Epstein, M. 1995. *Thoughts without a thinker: Psychotherapy from a Buddhist perspective*. New York: Basic Books.

Faure, B. 1993. *Ch'an insights and oversights: An epistemological critique of the Ch'an tradition*. Princeton: Princeton University Press.

Freud, S. 1993. *Three case histories*. Edited by Philip Rieff. New York: Collier.

Friedman, L. 1980. Kohut: A book review essay. *Psychoanalytic Quarterly* 49:393–422.

Golomb, E. 1992. *Trapped in the mirror: Adult children of narcissists in their struggle for self*. New York: William Morrow.

Hall, D. 1989. *Worlds of wonder, days of judgment: Popular religious belief in early New England*. New York: Alfred A. Knopf.

Harrison, S. 1997. *Doing nothing: Coming to the end of the spiritual search*. New York: Jeremy P. Tarcher/Putnam.

Hendricks, H. 1998. Confucius, the Tao, the ancestors, and the Buddha: The religions of China. In *Course Guide to The Great Courses on Tape, Part IV*. Springfield: The Teaching Company.

Hillman, J. 1983. *Healing fiction*. Barrytown, N.Y.: Station Hill Press.

Hoover, T. 1977. *Zen culture*. New York: Vintage Books.

Johansson, R. 1969. *The psychology of nirvana*. Garden City: Doubleday.

Jung, C. 1959. *Aion: Researches into the phenomenology of the self.* 2nd ed. Princeton: Princeton University Press.

Kohut, H. 1977. *The restoration of the self.* New York: International Universities Press.

———. 1984. *How does analysis cure?* Chicago: University of Chicago Press.

Lao Tzu. 1990. *Tao te ching: The classic book of integrity and the way.* Translated by V. Mair. New York: Bantam Books.

———. 1992. *Wen-tzu: Understanding the mysteries.* Translated by T. Cleary. Boston: Shambhala.

Lattimore, R. 1960. *Greek lyrics.* Chicago: University of Chicago Press.

Lesser, E. 1999. *The new American spirituality: A seeker's guide.* New York: Random House.

Lind, R. 1999. *The devil's due.* Rockville: Kabel, 1999.

Lothane, Z. 1992. *In defense of Schreber: Soul murder and psychiatry.* Hillsdale: Analytic Press.

Luther, M. 1957. *The bondage of the will.* New Jersey: Fleming H. Revell.

Mair, V. 1990. Afterword. In Lao Tzu, *Tao te ching: The classic book of integrity and the way.* New York: Bantam Books.

McGreal, I., ed. 1995. *Great thinkers of the Eastern world.* New York: HarperCollins.

Nussbaum, M. 1986. *The fragility of goodness: Luck and ethics in Greek tragedy and philosophy.* Cambridge: Cambridge University Press.

———. 1994. *The therapy of desire: Theory and practice in Hellenistic ethics.* Princeton: Princeton University Press.

O'Hear, A. 1999. *After progress: Finding the old way forward.* New York: Bloomsbury.

Ramaswami, S., and A. Sheikh. 1989. Buddhist psychology: Implications for healing. In *Healing East and West: Ancient wisdom and modern psychology,* edited by A. Sheikh and K. Sheikh. New York: John Wiley.

Rohde, E. 1966. *Psyche: The cult of souls and belief in immortality among the Greeks.* New York: Harper & Row.

Roof, W. 1999. *Spiritual marketplace: Baby boomers and the remaking of American religion.* Princeton: Princeton University Press.

Rose, N. 1990. *Governing the soul: The shaping of the private self.* New York: Routledge.

Schatzman, M. 1971. Paranoia or persecution: The case of Schreber. *Family Process* 10:177–212.

Seligman, M. 1993. *What you can change and what you can't: The complete guide to successful self-improvement.* New York: Alfred A. Knopf.

Singer, J., and P. Salovey. 1993. *The remembered self: Emotion and memory in personality.* New York: Free Press.

Taylor, C. 1989. *Sources of the self: The making of modern identity.* Cambridge: Harvard University Press.

Tuan, Y. 1998. *Escapism.* Baltimore: Johns Hopkins University Press.

Vitousek, K., and L. Ewald. 1993. Self-representation in eating disorders: A cognitive perspective. In *The self in emotional distress: Cognitive and psychodynamic theories,* edited by Z. Segal and S. Blatt. New York: Guilford Press.

Wesley, J. 1960. *A plain account of Christian perfection.* London: Epworth Press.

Index

① What's
new -
Paving
(on site)

② Midwinter, after holiday

phone link

✓ evans, ellen
∴ (benar chert)
✓ murdayle :
✓ king ?
✓ quirk ?
(anner)
ck. links

8 week study - chp' review
@ (lunch day) - wkly
$9 clinic session *

③ book study (w/ Kealy) -
8 weeks a house ?
every ___ (noha) night) weds ?
(6 people) @ $5. e